Developmental Tasks For Children, Adolescents & Adults

A Full Picture of Internal Development from Self-worth & Emotional Safety to Integrating Love, Truth, Beauty & Wisdom

Paul Hatherley

BALBOA.
PRESS
A DIVISION OF HAY HOUSE

Balboa Press books may be ordered through booksellers or by contacting:

Balboa Press
A Division of Hay House
1663 Liberty Drive
Bloomington, IN 47403
www.balboapress.com
1 (877) 407-4847

Because of the dynamic nature of the Internet, any web addresses or
links contained in this book may have changed since publication and
may no longer be valid. The views expressed in this work are solely those
of the author and do not necessarily reflect the views of the publisher,
and the publisher hereby disclaims any responsibility for them.

The author of this book does not dispense medical advice or prescribe the use
of any technique as a form of treatment for physical, emotional, or medical
problems without the advice of a physician, either directly or indirectly. The
intent of the author is only to offer information of a general nature to help
you in your quest for emotional and spiritual well-being. In the event you use
any of the information in this book for yourself, which is your constitutional
right, the author and the publisher assume no responsibility for your actions.

Any people depicted in stock imagery provided by Thinkstock are
models, and such images are being used for illustrative purposes only.
Certain stock imagery © Thinkstock.

Printed in the United States of America.

ISBN: 978-1-4525-1692-9 (sc)
ISBN: 978-1-4525-1694-3 (hc)
ISBN: 978-1-4525-1693-6 (e)

Library of Congress Control Number: 2014910750

Balboa Press rev. date: 06/11/2014

Contents

CONTENTS

Part III: Developmental Tasks for Adults

Foreword

At its most basic, life can be defined as *ceaseless motion in a context of unrelenting change*. For human beings, determining when life begins is currently controversial, but for the sake of this discussion let's say life begins when we slide down the birth canal and emerge into the glaring light with a gasp for air, immediately followed by a loud cry for someone, preferably mom, to feed our needs! So begins a lifelong struggle to survive, feed our needs and gratify desires, while we also move thru a lifespan doing our best to ignore, deny, or just distract ourselves away from acknowledging the fact that every creature born into life is pre-destined to die.

If we acknowledge that every birth, including ours, is eventually followed by death, no exceptions, then we need to ask: "What do we want to do with the time between our birth and death?" Not an easy question to answer! I first posed this question when at five, my grandmother died and I realized with shock and terror that I too, would die. This sad event began a lifetime of searching for the answer to my next question, "Since I am already alive and can't un-ring that bell: *what, if anything, will make my life, or anyone's life — satisfying, worthwhile, and meaningful?*"

I

A half-century, plus a decade and some change later, I have an answer. The problem is that my answer is not simple. So I can't say, "Take a vow of poverty, meditate, pray, believe in God or the Universe, or even *love* is everything." Trust me, at this point I wish there was a simple answer. Instead, there are *layers of answers* that start by organizing the complex experience of life beginning with the *basic fact* that each and every human is the proud owner of a *mind, body, emotions and lifespan.*

In addition to the basic facts, each life can be divided into *three segments — personal, relationships, and profession —* and within each *segment of life* and *basic fact* are *internal* needs and potentials that we must understand, feed, and fulfill: that is, if we want our lives to be satisfying, meaningful, and worthwhile.

The problem is that throughout human history our species has been obsessed with struggling and competing trying to control *external* security, approval, success, and if possible, luxury. We have left everything *internal* to our beliefs, feelings, religions, spiritual intuitions, and all things subjective, vague, and general. What I have done is to identify and experientially define all the *objective* and *universal* needs and potentials necessary to make our lives *internally* satisfying and permanently meaningful.

The good news is that since each step in the layers of awareness and skill necessary to master internal needs and potentials is now *experientially* defined, anyone who wants a meaningful life can build one to his unique specifications.

The bad news is that no matter how smart someone is, internal development is a big job, and can't be completed in a week. The thing to remember is that Mother Nature loves balance, so with every bit of good news there is always a bit of bad news. Once we accept this fact we can stop arguing with Mother Nature and get on with the job of acquiring all the layers of awareness and skill necessary to feed the needs and fulfill the potentials Mama Nature was ever so kind, and mean, as to bestow upon our unsuspecting heads.

Anyone who wants life to be *internally* and *externally* fulfilled has to define and complete every developmental task beginning with *emotional safety, self-worth, and self-awareness*. Then, we need to define *conscious purposes*, as well as *internal needs and potentials*. In this process, we also learn how to be a *satisfying mate, competent parent and real friend*. Finally, we need to master the activities of *expressing love, pursuing truth, experiencing beauty and developing wisdom*.

Internal tasks begin in childhood when our personalities are formed. For most people, childhood training is woefully inadequate, so we move into adolescence internally hungry, hormonally driven, lost and confused but still trying to pretend that we "know it all." As adolescents, we suffer from not having mastered emotional security and self-worth, and rather than becoming *self-aware,* are usually just *self-absorbed.* Without the foundation of having completed our childhood developmental tasks, in adolescence our responsibilities start to pile-up as we need to define ourselves, choose a career, relate to the opposite sex, and deal with internal needs.

III

With normal training, most adolescents don't have the slightest idea how to define their hungers or responsibilities, and neither do their parents, so we just muddle through this stage of life the best we can, and then move on to adult tasks where once again our responsibilities and internal hungers keep on accumulating — while our lack of internal development prevents us from understanding and completing many if not most of them.

As adults, we need to learn how to create intimacy and emotional bonds in long-term romantic relationships, as well help our children feed their internal needs for emotional safety, self-worth, and self-awareness. Of course, when we have not mastered these basic internal tasks for ourselves, it is impossible to help our children.

Later, when our children become adolescents we are often distracted by an unsatisfying relationship with our mate, absorbed by the demands of our career, and have neither the time nor developmental competence to respond effectively to the internal needs of adolescent children. Hence, the birth of a "generation gap" that is so common it has become a sad cliché, and is one reason we are rarely able to fulfill the human potential to *understand, care, master* and *create* for ourselves, and then *contribute* to the growth of other people.

The normal experience of growing from child to adult without the internal training necessary to complete our developmental tasks is one reason human life is not improving, but instead, is becoming more difficult, complicated, and at least internally, less satisfying rather than more fulfilling.

IV

Completing our developmental tasks in a sequential and time appropriate manner is essential to growing-up with our self-worth and emotional safety complete, and to acquire the skills and awareness necessary to create our own fulfillment, build emotional bonds, and over time, contribute to the evolution of our species. One consequence of internal education is that we discover a new world of mental and emotional needs and potentials that had previously been unknown, invisible, and beyond our capacity to see or understand.

In completing developmental tasks we learn to feed our *minds truth* and *emotions beauty*, and become competent to engage any problem and *think* about it until we *understand in detail* what is true and needed, and we learn how to nurture. Thru this process, we learn that *adult* self-worth is based on becoming internally and externally competent. We also learn that creating self-worth in a *child* is a different process, and requires parents who are competent to *acknowledge* a child rather than *approve*, and who understand themselves and life and have mastered their own developmental tasks.

Perhaps the greatest change that occurs as a result of internal development is that our reason for living is re-formed. Where once our greatest ambition was to lead a secure and pleasant life pretending that our lives do not end, and believing that success, approval, entertainment and great sex make life as complete as possible, we create a new vision. Now we see that mastering internal needs and potentials and integrating love, truth, beauty and wisdom are required for a whole-hearted existence that is meaningful and noble.

V

In this commercial age where the smart people join with the corporate mentality and support limitless exploitation for no greater purpose than amassing large sums of money for power and pleasure, an innocent desire for a noble life may seem quaint, old-fashioned, and irrationally out of step.

Indeed, a desire for integrity, nobility, love and wisdom, is sharply out of step with the overwhelming momentum of our times. If we study history, we soon see that a desire to create a noble existence has never been popular, but today, with the power of technology shaping everyone's thoughts, feelings, desires and vision of life, human beings are rapidly being funneled into accepting a commercial vision of life based on motivation provided by fear and greed, and with our highest goal to feel financially secure, good about ourselves, and pursuing the illusion that pleasant or exciting feelings are all we need for lasting happiness.

Mastering developmental tasks takes us into a new and different world with a detailed awareness of what life really is, and requires. Now, we see what *motivated* Shakespeare, Beethoven, Michelangelo, Jesus, Buddha, Abraham Lincoln, Anne Frank, or Nelson Mandela. In seeing what motivated these and many other people who pursued a noble existence, we can share in their joy and suffering, triumph and tragedy, and understand their purposes, caring and commitment. These people may even become our dearest friends.

At the same time, we also learn how to understand and nurture the living, breathing people closest to us. We have no control over anyone else wanting internal development

VI

or a noble life badly enough to work for it, but we can always love life and other people even if we are not loved. One definition of a noble choice is to pursue a *conscious purpose* to express love—whether or not we are loved in return.

If nothing else, mastering our developmental tasks and creating internal fulfillment and lasting happiness makes life a surprising adventure where every day brings new insight and intense emotional experiences that plunge us into the heights and depths of what life and Mother Nature offers, and we are never bored. Not only are we never bored, but in the end we will not mournfully cry-out as my aunt did on her deathbed, "Is this all there is?"

Instead, we will know we have experienced all that life offers, fulfilled every potential, understood and shared with the greatest minds and hearts produced by human life, and through it all we consciously cared about every moment and never failed in our commitment to *express love, pursue truth, experience and create beauty, and develop wisdom.*

Part I

Developmental Tasks

Of Childhood

Self-Worth &
Emotional Safety

The two most significant and basic developmental tasks for children are self-worth and emotional safety. Of course, this is not something most children can do for themselves. Instead, children depend on being lucky enough to have internally developed parents who are competent to help them develop a complete and intact self-worth, as well as a solid base for feeling emotionally safe in an impersonal world that is often cold, indifferent, or even dangerous.

When children fail to develop self-worth and emotional safety, they usually spend the rest of their lives feeling insecure, doubting their value, and trying to create safety and value thru accomplishments, romance, money, social status, psychotherapy, distraction and approval. The problem is that once we miss the opportunity to establish our self-worth and safety as children, the only remedy is to first *understand* internal needs and potentials, and then become *competent* to feed and fulfill every one.

In an ideal world, most parents would be developed enough to understand internal needs, and competent to feed them in their children. What have you observed is true in your life: first as a child, and perhaps now as a parent? As a child, were your internal needs fed? Are you competent now to feed your own and a child's need for worth and safety?

Tragically, most people never learn how to master even their most basic internal needs for self-worth and emotional safety. The simple answer for how to create worth and safety in our adult lives is to master the five internal potentials to **understand, care, master, create and contribute,** and in the process also learn how to define and feed every internal and external need. Nothing to it!

Unfortunately, human history has shown that **simple answers to complex problems** never work, at least not for long. One reason is that each word in the simple answer above represents a complex web of awareness and skills we must acquire over time, step by step, and layer by layer. In this and my other four books on internal development are the specific steps and concrete layers of information people need to feed and fulfill every internal need and potential.

For now, however, we will define what is needed to feed a child's internal need for safety and worth, and in the process learn what we received or missed as children, and what we need to provide for ourselves as adults.

To begin, a child needs parents who truly understand self-worth and emotional safety, and can feed both in themselves. *When a child's parents truly like themselves and each other, and give their time and energy in a context of relaxed attention and whole-hearted interest, then the child has real experience that he is valued and loved, and feels emotionally safe due to the internal competence and genuine understanding of his parents.* What was your experience as a child? Does this describe what you received, or not?

First Steps

People have a very predictable response when I describe what is needed to feed their children's needs. That is, everyone immediately says, "Yes, but how do I actually do what you are saying?" Glad you asked! ***Step one is to recognize your own internal hunger to be seen, acknowledged, understood, and liked.*** *Hatherley's second principle of a conscious life states that, "You cannot feed a hunger in your child that you do not recognize in yourself."*

The reason for this principle is simple. To truly empathize with a hunger in your child (or mate, friend, or parent), you must have suffered from the same hunger in yourself. Without a similar experience, you can only imagine a child's hunger, and your response will be mechanical, or based on a technique. A far cry from being tender and compassionate, and motivated by suffering from a similar and perhaps unsatisfied hunger that in the past may have damaged you, but now, you have learned to feed for yourself.

How will being aware of your hunger to be seen, liked, acknowledged and understood make a difference? Simple, you will be more patient when your child (mate or friend), insists on receiving your energy and attention. You will also be more likely to *want* to give your attention even when no one is bold enough to insist on it! In addition, you will be aware that nodding, smiling and saying "Good job!", or some other normal but uninformative judgment is quite unsatisfying for both you and the other person.

Instead, you will practice asking questions that *explore* a child's experience, so he learns to *acknowledge* the *facts* of his experience, his *emotional responses*, and the *consequences*. You will also ask questions that explore the *needs, motivations, and feelings* of other people involved in your child's story, i.e. their *perspectives*. Of course, you will want to tailor the sophistication of your questions to the age and capacity of your unique child. There is no cookie-cutter formula here, you will need to consciously experiment and practice.

One way to determine the level of your child's awareness is to ask questions as you would an adult. Then, if your child gives you a blank look, or storms off, you know your question was too far over his head! So you back down, and try again. It is important to note that asking a question that is over your child's developmental head will not hurt him. It may irritate him, and he may temporarily think you are an idiot, but everyone survives and no one suffers real damage. Following this process, you soon see precisely what you can ask your child, and what you can't—works on husbands too!

My experience has been that most parent's *underestimate* their child's level of awareness. The reason is that most adults have no clue how to handle a child's internal needs, and in the name of "protecting" their children limit their conversations. This does nothing to protect the child, but it does protect parents from exploring the depths of their own understanding and competence. If it is of comfort, I have never seen any parent in danger of drowning from the depth of his/her internal understanding and competence.

Exploring a Child's Experience

One way to learn how to *explore* rather than criticize, judge, explain, or draw conclusions is through examples. For instance, one clear day in a rural setting a seven year old boy named Slater was riding his scooter down a steep hill. At the bottom of the hill was a six year old girl named Willa, standing with her bicycle. Slater's mother, Alison was nearby observing both her son and his cousin, Willa.

Bravely, Slater came screaming down the hill, but when he got to the bottom, Willa made a feint with her bicycle as if she was going to move in front of him. She did not actually block him, but her feint scared Slater, even though he held his course and was not hurt. Afterward, Slater shocked his mother by screaming at Willa, "I hate you!" The mother, Alison, was angry at Willa, and admonished her for her action. Also, she was shocked by the vehemence in her son's voice.

By this time Willa was acting concerned and Alison said to her son trying to elicit a little compassion, "Willa is really struggling now." and Slater replied, "Good, I want her to struggle." At this point Alison did not know how to proceed with either Willa, or Slater. If you were the adult here, how would you help these two children *explore* this event?

Most parents would want to *explain* to the two children the potential danger to Slater, chastise Willa for her action, get a promise to not do it again, and maybe try to calm Slater by getting him to "forgive" Willa, perhaps by saying "She didn't mean it." or, "She did not know what she was doing."

If this were a normal interaction, the adult would be doing most of the talking and the children would be looking put-upon, bored, or in Slater's case, just angry. The outcome would be that neither the children or the adult would learn anything new, and this dramatic event would disappear into history without touching, teaching, or changing anyone.

If the adult in this instance wanted to *understand* this event, she would have to *acknowledge* the facts and *explore* each child's perspective. To begin, we need to know a little about each child. Willa is a precocious six year old, and she knew very well that Slater was moving so fast he was nearly out of control, so her feint was going to at least scare him. Slater too is precocious, and usually the one directing things and feeling in control, which results in a subtle rivalry and ongoing competition between them.

In response, Alison could acknowledge to Willa, "I know you saw Slater coming down the hill nearly out of control — so what did you want to happen when you pretended to put your bike in his way?" She would need to be prepared for a sullen, "I don't know." and then reply, "Well, what you saw happen was that Slater was first frightened, and then angry. He was frightened because he felt in danger of being hurt. What do you suppose made him so angry?"

We do not know what Willa would say, but we can take whatever she does say and explore it further, or suggest, "Do you think Slater believes you did this on purpose to scare him, and that you enjoyed seeing him be upset?" (Willa has a history of playing tricks on her younger brother, Finch, to torment him, so this is not an unreasonable question.)

The point is that Willa is being given focused attention, and is *exploring* what happened rather than being chastised, explained to, preached at, or judged. In the process of exploring, some of Willa's motivations and purposes will be revealed, whether she likes it or agrees with it, or not. Willa will be learning that *acknowledgment* does not always feel good, but it does identify grains of truth, and she will see herself in more detail than she ever would if Alison only admonished her about what *not to do*.

Before leaving Willa to turn our attention on Slater, we would need to ask her, "How would you have felt if Slater had swerved because of your feint, and been hurt?" I would ask this question in a neutral tone to give Willa every chance to be honest, and to whatever she said I would follow up with another question, "What about it would have made you feel sad, happy, or whatever?" One thing Willa would learn is that if she is going to torment another child, she will in turn be mildly tormented by having to explore it in detail.

As an aside, this strategy works only if Willa also gets attention for *positive* and *neutral,* as well as negative events. We never want to pair attention only with *negative* events. If we do that, then the message the child gets is that if she/he wants attention, the best way to get it is to act out and do something negative.

Now it is Slater's turn for attention and time to acknowledge he was coming down the hill very fast and unprepared for Willa's feint, so Alison could ask, "Do you think Willa intended to scare you?" Being Slater, he will probably say "Yes." Then, another innocent question, "Do you think you might have wanted to impress her, and when she feinted with her bike and scared you it ruined the whole moment?" There is a grain of truth here important to both children, so it does not matter whether either one admits it or not, they will see that Alison understands something about their invisible motivations, and their ongoing but unspoken rivalry.

If Slater admits he did want to impress Willa, then Alison could explore the issue with more questions. If not, she could simply offer, "Well, if you did want to impress Willa, she certainly ruined it didn't she?" Then, Alison could add, "How do you feel about being scared by a six year old *girl*?" The reason for this question is that part of Slater's rage is feeling humiliated by a girl he wants to impress.

Slater and Willa are only seven and six, but already there are some male/female dynamics of competition and power going on. These dynamics are mostly unconscious and totally innocent, but significant because they are forming patterns that will continue in adult life.

The point of going through this process with the two children is to show them how to *explore for understanding* rather than judge, explain, criticize or conclude. In the process, they will learn how to *accurately describe the facts* of an event, *separate facts from feelings, identify motivations and purposes*, see *two perspectives*, and consciously try to build *understanding*, rather than take sides and assign blame. They will also experience the first step to experiencing real love, *learning*.

Consequences of Exploring

Perhaps surprisingly, teaching children how to explore by modeling it ourselves is a powerful tool in helping them develop self-worth and emotional security. It is also a secret key that opens the door to all the other dimensions of mental and emotional development. If there is one single cause for all the world's self-induced tragedy and trauma, it is the universal inability to explore reality, needs, and potentials until we *understand* them, and can respond competently.

On the other hand, if there is one single remedy for needless human trauma and tragedy, it is learning how to explore ourselves, life, needs, potentials, and other people's perspectives until we thoroughly understand every one. What we can learn from Slater and Willa's story is that if we give energy and attention, observe facts, ask questions, and teach children to think about and articulate their experience, we will model and teach a myriad of developmental tasks.

In our sample story, we not only acknowledged the facts, but we also explored the *internal* motivations, feelings, and purposes of both children, and we revealed our interest in *understanding* rather than *controlling*. This is opposite to a normal adult being primarily interested in trying to control the *external* aspects of a child's actions and attitudes, i.e., in this case, Willa's action and Slater's anger.

When a child experiences an adult genuinely wanting to understand rather than control, he/she immediately relaxes, and over time, will apply this process to himself.

One consequence of trying to *understand* rather than control is that the child drops judgment, and adopts curiosity. Now, the child develops a desire to learn about himself rather than judge, criticize, explain, or defend. This is critical to developing self-worth and emotional security, because the child learns that *exploring leads to understanding*, and *understanding* leads to a more satisfying experience of being alive.

In a normal *externally-based* life we expect our rewards to come from pleasure, approval, security and success. This is one reason we never create a file in our minds for wanting to patiently *explore experience until we understand it*. Sadly, we do not expect the *internal* experience of understanding either can, or will be satisfying, so we have no reason to spend the time and energy necessary to learn how to explore ordinary events and everyday reality.

Developing a *burning desire* to understand ourselves, life, and other people is itself a developmental task that changes our motivations, purposes, and priorities. Once we see both the need **and** reward for *understanding* internal motivations, needs, purposes and potentials, not only for ourselves, but also for our mates, friends, children and the entire human species, we create a *conscious purpose* for our lives that will transcend any desire for luxury, pleasure, approval, or the illusion of security.

When we teach children how to explore, and in the process they discover the joy of understanding, they become fearless in the face of emotional pain because they know that pain leads to learning — and learning leads to love.

Accurate Self-Awareness

Another developmental task of childhood, and critical to becoming fully human, is to develop *self-awareness*. Even the most intelligent animals like elephants, dolphins, whales, chimpanzees and guerillas have a limited self-awareness, in part, because they do not have language or writing, and their inability to measure time and restrictions in their ability to reason limit their imagination. For instance, elephants can acknowledge and mourn the actual death of other elephants, but cannot, as far as we know, like human beings imagine, anticipate, or worry about their own deaths.

Nor can other animals develop a *conscious internal life* where they use memory and reason to *picture* a past event, determine precisely what happened, define the specific *motivations and purposes* that drove their choices and behaviors, identify the consequences, see where they were *congruent vs. contradictory* and in the process learn about their *characters*. Only human beings have the *internal potential* for this degree of self-awareness, however, in my experience very few people develop this level of awareness.

When we fail to fulfill our uniquely human potential to become self-aware, we also fail to fulfill our potential to become compassionate, to understand our own best interest, and to master that most critical of developmental tasks— how to learn from experience.

<u>Who Am I?</u>

This is a question we first engage as infants, and then often spend the rest of our lives trying to answer. Early on, we become familiar with Mom and Dad, and identify them as our *special people*. Eventually, we understand they are responsible for us being alive, and we understand what the words Mom and Dad really mean. We also learn about gender, and determine whether we are a boy or girl.

It is important to observe that even the smartest animals never comprehend gender, or *consciously* understand family ties; these levels of *self-awareness* are limited to human beings. It is also important to notice that even human levels of self-awareness are primarily *external*, and most people never understand the *internal* dimensions defined by their needs, motivations, purposes and potentials.

Even *external* dimensions of self-awareness have significant consequences. For instance, at some time in childhood we become aware of our race, religion, and the social status we inherit from our parents. These external dimensions of self-awareness result in defining ourselves by statements like: "I am rich — or poor." or "I am Catholic — or Jewish."

When we learn about our parent's social status, and/or degree of material success, we often define ourselves in terms that mirror what becomes familiar in our home life, and has nothing whatever to do with our unique talents or innate preferences. This is one way we develop a *self-image* that sometimes creates a tragic degree of *self-limitation*!

However, the most tragic consequence of a distorted self-image comes from internal sources. For instance, developing self-worth and emotional security requires we begin with an accurate self-awareness that we *build on to* become competent to define, feed, and fulfill every internal need and potential. When we spend a lifetime struggling to just *feel* worthwhile and emotionally safe, then even if we are fully successful at acquiring every *external* aspect of the American Dream — *career-mate-house-family-three car garage and luxurious vacations* — we still fail to either understand or develop self-respect, internal fulfillment, or lasting happiness.

Motivations & Purposes

One way to teach children, and ourselves, how to begin answering the question, "Who am I?" is to observe and clearly define our *motivations* and *purposes*. If we return to the example of Willa and Slater from the last chapter, we can see that in exploring the event of Willa pretending she was going to block Slater's headlong descent on his scooter, we identified that Slater wanted to impress Willa with his physical stunt, while Willa let him know by her action that she was not going to be so easily impressed.

As the adult, we need to understand their motivations and purposes, so over time, we can help the children understand themselves. Before we begin, we need to first define *motivation* and *purpose* to see what makes them different. *Motivation* can be defined as the *catalyst* for our behavior. *Purpose*, on the other hand, is defined by our ultimate *goal*.

So in this instance, one of Slater's *motivations* was a desire to impress Willa and get her approval, but his unconscious *purpose* was to feel desirable and worthwhile. This specific combination of *motivation* and *purpose,* where we are *motivated* by a *longing for approval* and our *purpose* is to feel *desirable and worthwhile* is experienced by most children, and if we fail to complete our developmental tasks this process continues forever, and we remain unfulfilled for a lifetime.

The problem is that no one can ever get enough approval to create self-worth and become emotionally safe, because we *want* approval, but we *need* acknowledgement. As adults, the requirements change and we need to become *internally competent* to feed and fulfill our own needs and potentials.

In our story about Willa and Slater, Willa's motivation and purpose were similar to, and competitive with Slater's. While Slater wanted Willa's approval, Willa intuitively understood that if she gave Slater her approval, he would feel powerful and in-charge and she would not get the focused energy and attention she wanted. So at the tender age of six, she has seen that *withholding* approval is the best way to both retain her power, and keep the attention focused on her.

This is one lifetime pattern we often form in childhood, and then act out for the rest of our lives. Do you recognize it in yourself, or in other people? If you can see this pattern, then you will also understand what so often makes intimacy in adult relationships impossible. That is, we learn as children to compete for power and approval, which make us *adversaries* — not internally intimate and emotionally bonded.

__Develop Caring__

Though it is not obvious, *self-awareness, caring, and self-worth* are all consequences of completing *developmental tasks*. As children, we first acquire self-awareness through the eyes and attention of our parents. If our parents see us primarily in terms of external behaviors—whether we are good or bad, or whether we make them proud or ashamed—then we will see ourselves in terms of *external characteristics* and *behaviors*, and in terms of our parent's feelings and judgments.

Growing-up feeling that we are *good* or *bad*, and with our self-worth a reflection of our parent's feelings and judgments is normal. In fact, this normal process is the reason so many people go through life trying to prove their worth by getting approval, but then no matter how accomplished or successful they become it is never enough. The reason is we need parents to *acknowledge* both our strengths and weaknesses, so we can see ourselves accurately, rather than judge our value thru the lens of our parent's feelings and prejudices.

When our parents provide the energy and take the time to explore our experiences, thoughts, feelings, motivations and purposes on a regular basis we get practice observing ourselves, other people and life, so we learn how to identify facts, observe our responses, define the consequences, and learn from experience. *Thru this complex internal process, we experience our parents energy and focus, emotional support, and intelligent insight coming together to nurture us, and to our innocent young minds this proves we are loved.*

We all need *internal* proof of real love from our parents to develop a **whole-hearted caring** for ourselves, being alive, and for other people. In normal life, the best most people receive is *external* proof their parents love them, which is why we frequently fail to complete this basic developmental task — *whole-heartedly* loving ourselves and life.

Internal proof of love is the same for children as it is for adolescents and adults. The consistent *experience* of undivided interest, energy, time, focus, and intelligent attention proves to another person that we truly care about him/her. No amount of material things, financial support, or approval will ever make-up for the absence of an internal *experience* of real caring and genuine love.

Once we understand this fact, we will also understand why children from affluent homes so often grow-up entitled rather than grateful, and why wives of successful husbands are also frequently angry or entitled, rather than grateful. The reason is that we all have external needs for survival, but emotional bonds and lasting happiness can be built only on internal fulfillment. **Whoever learns how to provide internal fulfillment will be both loving and loved, and whoever does not will never experience a full measure of either one.**

This last *principle of life* is easily observed once you know what to look for. Until then, we often search for love, but find that it is an elusive thing we can never define or discover in either ourselves, or other people. First choice is to be born to *internally developed* parents who can acknowledge us, second choice is to master this basic need for ourselves.

Internal Needs

Developing *self-worth, self-awareness and emotional safety* feeds critical *internal needs* found in children, adolescents, and adults. These needs are *internal* because they arise out of possessing *minds and emotions,* and if we fail to feed them, then we suffer mental and emotional damage. These needs evolve in each *stage of development* in terms of complexity, and who is responsible to feed them. In children, parents are responsible, and if parents receive training and complete their own development, a child's needs are fairly simple.

Without training, parents soon discover that the internal needs of children are intangible and invisible, and they have little or no chance of identifying, defining, or feeding them.

The problem for most families is that the parents have neither the training or development necessary to feed their children's internal needs, so almost everyone grows-up ignorant of how to define and feed their needs for self-worth, self-awareness, and emotional safety. This is one reason that tension, anxiety, chronic discontent and depression, or in general just being neurotic is a *normal* state of mind for a large majority of the American population.

The source for this widespread *normal neurosis* is that a *hungry animal is a tense and anxious animal,* and as a culture, Americans are *externally* satiated, but *internally* starving. As complicated as external poverty and hunger is to resolve, internal poverty is many times more difficult. At least we can see external hunger, the internal variety is invisible.

One way to make internal needs visible is to **define them in terms of experience.** For instance, *self-worth* can be defined as the *experience of our value based first on having parents who feed our internal and external needs, and then as adults by becoming competent to feed every real need for ourselves.* In addition, adults need to fulfill their internal and external *potentials* before their self-worth will be both permanent and complete.

Self-awareness can be defined as developing a *conscious ability* to **accurately** *observe our strengths and weaknesses, needs and potentials, contradictions and congruence, as well as every strength and inadequacy.* As children, we need parents to feed this need, but as with every other real need, as adults we must learn to feed ourselves. Adolescence is a time of transition where step by step and layer by layer, our task is to consciously acquire the internal competence to feed ourselves.

Developing emotional safety in childhood requires that *our parents have the ability to see reality accurately, respond competently, and thoroughly understand our needs and potentials.* As adults, we must develop our own internal competence, so *emotional safety* is the result of being able to trust ourselves to see reality accurately and create our own internal fulfillment.

If the three internal needs of self-worth, self-awareness and emotional safety are fed by our parents, then we lay the cornerstone for creating a *conscious and satisfying internal life,* or if deprived, we often develop a character that is to some degree forever anxious, divided, or discontent. Understanding this *developmental process* makes it possible to change our characters, and fulfill our potential for lasting happiness.

Emotional Warmth

Everyone is at least vaguely aware there are differences between a *warm* experience with another person that is in fact personal, satisfying and connected, and a *cold* interaction that leaves us lonely and isolated; or even rejected, criticized, or devalued. What everyone does not consciously consider is to think about warm versus cold experiences to determine precisely what creates them, and then note the consequences to our own mental and emotional states, to the other person, and to the relationship.

Warmth is important at every stage of life, but it is critical to our internal development in childhood. For a child, experiencing warmth from his parents makes the difference between developing emotional safety and self-worth, or enduring a lifetime of feeling insecure in his value, emotionally unsafe, and chronically anxious. Most parents intend to be warm toward their children, and some are successful in being *externally* warm, but few parents understand *internal* warmth or know how to express it, so most children grow-up suffering some degree (mild to severe) of chronic anxiety or fearfulness, and an inadequate level of self-worth.

In fact, many psychologists have told me that *working on self-worth* is inevitably a *lifetime project*. To me, that only makes self-worth a needless and painful *lifetime limitation*.

Emotionally Warm vs. Cold

What sometimes makes warm and cold hard to identify is they take place on both *external* and *internal* dimensions of experience, and both are subject to being misinterpreted because some experiences can *appear* or *feel* warm, but in *fact* be cold—and vice versa. So let's define the experience of warm vs. cold on internal and external dimensions, and identify the similarities and differences between an *image* or *feeling* of emotional warmth or coldness, and what in *fact* is true.

For a child, *external warmth* is defined by physical and material nurturing. Physical warmth is expressed by holding, hugging, patting, or putting our arm around a child—when he is hungry for the experience (important caveat!). Providing material warmth requires that parents be enthusiastic about feeding a child's external needs for clothing, food, shelter, education, etc. The combination of physical and material nurturing in a context of *conscious caring and offered with a joyful commitment* will feed a child's external needs, and will create a consistent experience of warmth that will convince a child he is emotionally safe and truly valued.

Most parent's understand the last paragraph and try to provide its requirements, and some do. Even if successful, however, the job is still only half done. Also, one difficult condition in offering to feed even external needs is the pesky *"context of conscious caring and joyful commitment."* To help you assess this difficulty simply ask, "How often have I done anything with *conscious caring and a joyful commitment?"*

Providing for a child's external needs offers one example of how an *internal* component, or condition, can make or break what *should* be a warm experience. In this case, we see how offering external nurturing without the internal component of conscious caring and joyful commitment creates only an *image of warmth,* which in reality is experienced as painfully cold, contradictory and confusing.

If anyone is interested, this is one way children from what seem to be *loving homes* can become mass murderers, and how everyone can be mystified *"How could that happen?"* This process also shows how children and adults who *have it all* can be miserable in a way that no one understands. On the other hand, if there is enough material wealth to feed basic needs, and parents nurture each other and the children in a *context of conscious caring and joyful commitment,* then the parents can first build emotional bonds with each other, and then the children, so the children grow-up with their emotional safety and self-worth intact.

Can you now see that internal warmth, beginning with conscious caring and a joyful commitment, is more complicated than external nurturing and requires information and training to learn and master? Children need their parents to be internally and externally competent, but without training it rarely happens. For instance, can you define the difference between being *personal* and *impersonal,* and then identify the specific attitudes and behaviors that define both? If you can, then you will understand a critical component of internal warmth—and if not, read on and you will learn.

Internal Warmth

Learning how to be *personal* in thought, conversation, purpose, attitude and behavior is the first step in offering *internal warmth* to a child, mate, friend, or business associate. Can you see from this one-sentence description that offering warmth thru being *personal* must be a *conscious* pursuit, and over time, it will be integrated into who you are, what you think and care about, and into every attitude and behavior?

So what makes a conversation or behavior *personal* versus *impersonal*? First, if we acknowledge Hatherley's first law of human life that says, "Purpose Determines Outcome", and it is our *purpose* to increase *understanding* of ourselves, life and other people, then we will *think and care* about topics that are *significant* to our own and everyone else's real needs, internal development, and lasting happiness.

On the other hand, if our purpose is to *control* pain and pleasure, feel good about ourselves, acquire security, and to generally avoid investing energy and thought into life and other people, or even ourselves when there is no immediate reward of approval, money or pleasure, then we will unconsciously select *trivial or superficial* topics to think and talk about, so our interactions with other people will inevitably be *impersonal*, repetitive—and deadly dull boring!

Most people may not mind being impersonal, may even think it is essential to being polite and socially acceptable, but some may mind being *deadly dull boring*. If you do mind being boring, then we need to explore significant topics.

<u>Exploring Significant Topics</u>

Recently, Denise, a friend and Marriage & Family therapist, related that her thirty-something daughter remarked that her two children (Denise's grandchildren), are more relaxed and manageable when *Grandma* is around than when she isn't. The daughter then went on to say how much she is learning from workshops, therapy, etc. on how to handle the children, and yet, they are still very difficult.

Denise was complaining to me that her daughter did not seem to have the slightest clue that maybe the children's improved attitudes and behaviors were directly due to her influence. Denise was also hurt that her daughter never asked for advice or information, which left her wondering what was going on. This is an example of a significant topic that is *personal* to mother and daughter. (Even in our thirties, we are still our mother's child!)

In this case, we are looking at three generations, and sadly, in terms of internal development, no adults. Denise feels guilty about having been an inadequate mother, and does not want to discuss this topic with her daughter, but still feels a degree of hurt and resentment. Typical family issue, right? What could Grandma do? What would you do?

Do you think Grandma should tell her daughter about her hurt and resentment? If she does, it may well start a fight and make things worse. Even though most therapists would encourage us to express our hurts and resentments to our loved ones, I generally caution against it.

The reason I caution against expressing hurts and resentments is because our loved ones also have unexpressed hurts and resentments, and expressing ours unleashes theirs, and in the heat of the moment no one is prepared to explore the facts, everyone wants to be heard, but no one is listening! Have you ever experienced something similar to this painful and frustrating scenario?

What I suggest doing is explore the facts to understand the other person's perspective, especially those facts that will reveal the issue you feel hurt and resentful about. In this instance, I suggested that Denise ask her daughter, *"What do you think makes your children more relaxed and manageable when I am here, than when I am not?"* Now, rather than *telling* her daughter about her feelings, or advising her daughter on how she should be, think or act, Denise is *asking* for her observations and opinions about a significant topic.

What would you rather experience: being told, criticized or complained to—or innocently asked what you see and think? Of course, one question only opens a topic, next Denise might ask, *"Does it seem to you that I give your children more warmth and understanding than I gave you?* This question opens the door for a possible flood of feelings. In preparing for this flood, Denise needs to be willing to acknowledge her daughter's hurt and anger, and take responsibility for both.

For instance, *after* exploring her daughter's feelings in excruciating detail, Denise might say, *"You are correct in assessing me as inadequate to feed your childhood internal needs, and even some of your external needs, and I am truly sorry. I have no defense, but it might help you understand yourself and me to know that I did not receive internal warmth or understanding as a child either. I have only learned in recent years how to provide warmth and understanding, and your children respond to me because they are as hungry for these experiences as you were as a child, and as you are now as an adult. My only hope is that you could learn from me now how to provide warmth and understanding for yourself first, and then your children, and in the process learn how to receive and share it with me. Would you like to try?*

Though many years have passed and the daughter is now herself an adult, the pain of her childhood was never acknowledged and understood, so is still fresh. As a result, the daughter continues to be angry, and sadly, is now herself *internally* inadequate in being a mother. If Denise uses questions to bring out her daughter's hurts and resentments, then the poison that contaminates their relationship can finally be consciously acknowledged, explored, and understood.

Through a *conscious* process of *exploring significant topics*, Mother and Daughter can start anew with a conscious desire to learn from their experience. However, if Denise focuses on expressing her hurts and resentments, gives advice, or makes demands, her daughter will be further frustrated and they will become more distant from each other than ever. The latter scenario is normal and happens in nearly every home in degrees from mild to severe. The former scenario is what everyone needs, but it requires a sophisticated degree of internal development and a high level of training to fully implement.

Feeding a Child's Internal Needs

The source of the internal warmth necessary to complete our childhood developmental tasks is having parents who competently feed our internal needs. So far, we have seen that if parents help us explore ordinary experience and discover what is true, engage us in personal interactions, and are truly competent to understand our motivations, needs, purposes and behaviors, then they create an internally warm environment necessary for us to develop emotional safety, self-worth, and an accurate self-awareness. In the next step, we will expand our inquiry to further define a child's internal needs and open the door to learning how to feed them.

First and foremost, children need to be *acknowledged **and understood*** with all their positive, negative and neutral characteristics in *experiential* detail. Most parents are trained to offer either positive judgments: "Great job! Your amazing! Such a good kid!" or critical ones; "You never think! You are so selfish! You can't ever do anything right!" etc.etc. Do any of these sound familiar?" Do you see what is missing in both critical and positive judgments?

What is missing is accurate information. A judgment is a global assessment based on someone's prejudice, opinion, or emotional reactions and gives no useable information, is cold as ice, and if delivered by our parents leaves us feeling undesirable, of no value, invisible, and often angry.

By contrast, an acknowledgment is personal, descriptive and factual, and proves we are thought about and valued.

Through acknowledgment we learn to accurately assess our development, so we can appreciate the value of what we do well, and be relaxed about our weaknesses. We also become competent to learn from experience, which means we can turn failure, success, loss, joy and pain into life lessons that provide critical information on how to understand internal needs and potentials. In the process, we work toward completing our childhood developmental tasks and adopt a lifetime purpose to become ever more loving and wise.

However, we need our parents to acknowledge much more than just our unique strengths and weaknesses, we also need our parents to acknowledge their own struggles, the facts, feelings, and events that define ordinary life, as well as help us understand the developmental levels and individual characters of the many varieties of people in the world.

The purpose for acknowledging is so we can learn how to consciously observe, ask questions, and understand ourselves, our parents, other people, and the mysterious reality of just being alive. It is thru the development of a detailed awareness that we create an *active internal life* worthy of possessing human potentials. Based on the depth and breadth of our *internal lives* we create the lasting satisfaction and permanent meaning necessary for our personal fulfillment, interpersonal intimacy, and long-term human happiness.

When parents lead us into exploring the full spectrum of daily life, and we walk together sharing the known and unknown, our relationship becomes warm, safe and satisfying, our internal needs are fed, and our potentials defined.

Internal Education

Everyone understands that children need education. As a result, we all acknowledge the obvious fact that children must be taught how to speak, socialize with other children, how to share, and how to distinguish right from wrong. The fact that children also need formal schooling in how to read, write, do arithmetic, etc., is also obvious to everyone. What is not so obvious is that children need a ***conscious education in how to be internally human.***

For instance, children need to learn the difference between *external* and *internal* dimensions of everyday life. They also need to see how *needs* are different from *wants*, how to *think for the purpose of understanding*, how to identify the *internal potentials* that make them human, how to define *conscious purposes*, and how to identify their own and other people's *attitudes, purposes, needs, motivations and priorities*.

These are observable examples of the layers of internal development necessary to grow-up emotionally secure with an accurate self-awareness, a complete self-worth, and the initial skills necessary to explore everyday life and discover for ourselves what is true and needed. In the past, there has been no detailed and clearly defined structure for teaching the internal awareness and skills necessary for every child to develop a truly sophisticated level of consciousness, wholehearted caring, and internal competence.

For parents to teach the internal awareness and skills children must have to complete their developmental tasks, we must first educate the adults, so they in turn can teach their children. The only problem with this approach is that we have to challenge the veracity of the age-old cliché, *"you can't teach old dogs new tricks."* Oh well, I never did put much stock in clichés, even the ancient *tried and true* ones!

Developing a Desire to Understand

The first step in educating both adults and children is to develop a *desire to understand.* Children are instinctually curious, and usually have an innocent desire to understand life that parents all too often unintentionally extinguish. What happens is that parents want children to learn all the "right answers" to predictable questions about what is right, wrong, good and bad. In addition, normal parents usually offer approval or disapproval rather than acknowledgment, so children quickly learn that if they want approval they must be "good" and acquire all the "right" answers, while they must avoid difficult, disturbing, or painful questions.

In the competition for approval children lose innocence and curiosity, and replace them with rigid ideas and beliefs. If you think about what we teach children about life, death, happiness, and romantic relationships; what do you see? Do you see parents encouraging their children to be aware of life, and the meaning of death? Or, do you see parents *protecting* their children from disturbing or painful realities?

In the name of *protecting* children from painful reality, we teach them to avoid any and all internally or externally painful experiences. We also teach children that the highest goal of life is to "enjoy it". If we observe most parents, we see the normal idea of a good life is defined by following the pattern of establishing a well-paying career, so we can mate and procreate, retire into a state of leisure, and finally, we hope to be lucky enough to die quietly in our sleep at a ripe old age. Through it all, we want to live in a state of unbroken and *controlled pleasantness*. So, what's the problem?

There is no problem, as long as we don't want to fulfill our human potentials, or create conscious and meaningful purposes, or experience the satisfaction of mastering internal needs, or know the joy and peace of building emotionally bonded relationships, or the personal fulfillment provided by an intimate connection to life, love, and wisdom. As long as we are content to spend life working for survival and entertaining ourselves, then *controlled pleasantness* is enough.

If we want something more, then education is required, and it begins with developing a *desire to understand* that reawakens the instinctual innocent curiosity we are all born with, but is so quickly extinguished by the normal *desire to control* pain and pleasantness, security, and approval.

To see this critical choice in experiential detail requires defining what we value, not in terms of our self-image, but by *observing* our everyday priorities, topics of conversation, and degree of competence to create personal and professional fulfillment, and intimate emotional bonds.

Becoming Observation-Based

Replacing a *normal desire to control* with a *conscious desire to understand* is the first *new trick* us *old dogs* must learn—if we want to teach children how to be happy and internally fulfilled human beings. Building on a *burning desire to understand,* the second trick we must learn as normally trained adults is how to *replace* our traditional reliance on beliefs and feelings with learning how to observe, ask questions, and use reason to build personal, detailed, and accurate pictures of ourselves, life, and other people.

In normal life, we teach children to *believe* in religions, right and wrong, good and bad, democracy and capitalism, which are all *ideas* about life and how we think it should be structured and lived. In addition, we frequently teach small children to believe in the fantasy of Santa Claus, the Easter Bunny, and the Tooth Fairy. (I was a rabid fan of all three!)

We also teach children to believe in the romantic fantasy of *falling in love* and *living happily ever after,* i.e. the fairy tales of Snow White, Cinderella, etc. These last two fairy tales we support throughout life by way of books, magazines, romantic movies, and a generally accepted cultural fantasy.

One destructive consequence of *normal education* is that we learn to rely on *concepts, beliefs, or feelings* for a picture of reality, rather than simply *observing* our parents, culture, peers, and everyday experience. The problem is that ideas, beliefs and feelings are *friends of control*, but frequently conflict with the *accurate observations* that lead to understanding.

The source of the fundamental conflict between relying on observations versus normal ideas, beliefs and feelings is that the *warmth of understanding* requires the *flexible accuracy* we obtain by being *observation-based*, while the *coldness of control* builds on the *rigidity and distortions* created by ideas, beliefs and feelings that are by definition always *out of sync* with current facts and needs.

If we want to be connected to the experience of being alive, and want to build an innocent and conscious internal life with a mind that is developmentally capable of empathy and compassion and competent to offer the warmth of true understanding, then we must teach *our old minds the new trick* of being observation-based. We must also become skillful at asking questions, using reason to connect cause and effect, and then experiment with our new insight to discover anew, in each moment, precisely what is true and needed.

I know this may sound daunting and like a lot of work, but once you get started you may find *it's so damn satisfying* there is nothing else you would rather spend your time and energy doing. The process of becoming observation-based and learning how to ask questions, use reason, and experiment with the innocent purpose of wanting to understand is the foundation for creating all the experiences we previously *believed* should happen, or *fantasized* would happen if we just found the right person, won the lottery, believed in the right religion, became rich and famous, blah, blah, blah!

Now that we have a foundation, let's see if we can apply it to a number of popular and well-known human issues.

Emotional Bonding

The first thing parent's unintentionally teach us is the depth and limits of their ability to bond emotionally. We are probably most bonded with our parents during infancy when everyone thinks we are cute, our mobility is limited, and our needs are largely self-evident and mostly external. As we grow older, however, our complex internal needs become more dominant, and since our parents rarely have the necessary training, their ability to offer a satisfying emotional bond usually diminishes with each passing year.

One consequence is that even if we are well-cared for physically, most of us grow-up with little or no experience for how to offer or receive a genuine emotional bond. Instead, our parents and teachers normally offer ideas, beliefs and expectations about emotional bonds, but no real understanding of what is required, and no personal experience.

An example of normal training is seen in the story of a seven year old boy, Slater, listening to his teacher read a story about a young prince who meets a beautiful young princess, falls in love at first sight, and wants to marry her. After the story, the teacher asks the children how they felt about it, and almost every child expressed approval and delight. Only Slater said that he thought the prince was stupid. The teacher asked Slater what he meant, and he said, "The prince knew the princess for one day — and he wants to marry her?" The teacher replied, "Well, she was so beautiful." and Slater says, "What does that matter? He doesn't know her!"

Hearing a piece of wisdom coming from one lone seven year old is both heartening and sad. Sad, because this whole classroom of children is being taught to see adult love as superficial, impersonal, and defined by external criteria. This example was also heartening because one boy was *observation-based* and stated the obvious issue that marrying someone we do not know based on physical attraction is by definition, "stupid." The reason is Hatherley's first law of life, "Purpose Determines Outcome."

This law reveals that if we begin a romantic relationship based on trivial criteria, then we have no chance of creating a satisfying or meaningful emotional bond. It cannot happen. Nonetheless, we continue to believe in love at first sight, and that a lifetime of passion can be based on superficial criteria. This belief is just about as rational as believing we can win the lottery even though we never buy a ticket. Of course, even if we do buy a ticket our chances don't dramatically increase, at least not by any mathematical standard.

The problem is that if we do not buy a lottery ticket then our odds are mathematically certain that we will not win. On the other hand, if we buy a ticket, our odds of winning are so infinitesimal that failure is still almost certain. The same is true when we choose a mate based on trivial criteria. That is, it is *almost certain* we cannot create a satisfying or meaningful emotional bond. Sadly, this principle also holds true in that we have no better odds for creating a warm and understanding relationship with our children when the relationship is based on superficial and external criteria.

So what do we need? We need parents who understand that *acknowledging* a child's strengths and weaknesses is a *personal* and satisfying interaction for both child and parent. We also need parents who understand that *acknowledging* the facts of life, the *requirements* for emotional bonding, the *reality* of internal needs, and the *process* necessary to fulfill our human potentials is required to provide children with the *internal education* necessary to complete their developmental tasks.

<u>Understanding Love</u>

A *normal* education teaches that love is *understood* to be a sentimental or instinctual feeling, or a consequence of desire, such as the prince in our story felt for the beautiful princess, or real-life women sometimes feel toward the lifestyle, social status, and security they hope the man of their choice will provide. Of course, woe unto the man if he fails to provide the expected benefits, or to a woman if she becomes over-weight, or when normal aging makes her beauty fade!

In stark contrast, a *conscious* education teaches that love is complex, requires internal development to experience and express, and must be studied in detail until we *understand* the levels and layers of attitudes, awareness, and actions that make-up a satisfying and meaningful experience of real love.

So much for the normal *belief* that we can *fall in lust and live happily ever after.* Oh well, if a seven year old boy with no training can see thru the silliness of that belief, maybe with a little training intelligent adults can too!

Loving a child begins with offering internal and external warmth. *External warmth,* we previously identified as feeding a child's material needs, as well as the need for physical affection as expressed thru appropriate and conscious touching. The internal portion needed to make this external experience truly loving is created by our attitude. So if we feed a child's *external* needs with an *internal* attitude defined by *conscious caring and joyful commitment,* then we establish a base-line of real love. However, the benefit from external nurturing can be ruined if we offer it with an attitude of obligation, indifference, or with conditions—like the famous old cliché, *"If you eat at my table, then you follow my rules."*

External nurturing offered in a context of conscious caring and joyful commitment provides the most basic level of warmth that children need to begin completing the developmental tasks defined by emotional safety and self-worth. The next step is for parents to become competent to *educate* a child in how to *understand* the *experience of love* by *modeling* it! This is where the real work begins, and we quickly discover who wants to *understand* himself, life and other people, and who is committed to *controlled pleasantness.*

Becoming competent to educate a child in how to understand the experience of real love requires that we first educate ourselves. For instance, the young female teacher who was educating her class to *believe* that love is an instinctual feeling that is often the consequence of a desire as primitive as lust, must first learn for herself the layers and levels of internal development necessary for real love to exist.

*The learning process for our young teacher, or anyone, begins with an **innocent desire to understand** rather than **control**.* The next step is to learn how to *observe* the facts of a specific event or circumstance, identify what they mean, and discover what is needed in each new situation. In the process, we need to ask intelligent questions, use reason to connect cause and effect, and experiment with each new insight until we understand every real need and potential. These initial steps require training and practice. One critical source of training is acquired by reading and studying this and my other four books on internal development.

Another critical source of internal training is to teach yourself to *observe* ordinary life until you are familiar with the facts that define human existence. For example, simple observation quickly teaches that all human life ends in death, which basically scares the pants off everybody (even though some of us deny it). By observing, we also soon learn that everyone feels hungry for the warmth provided by acknowledgment and understanding. Finally, observing everyday life reveals we are all internally hungry to understand and share this frightening mystery of being alive.

These observations reveal universal hungers, or internal needs that all human beings share in common, and acquiring insight into these needs and hungers creates a foundation for understanding the complex experience of real love. Remember, real love requires we feed internal needs, which is impossible if we can't define even one! Next, we will apply this initial description of internal needs to feeding them.

Feeding Internal Needs

A child must actually experience his/her internal needs being fed to understand they even exist. This difficult prerequisite holds true for adults too. Our task as adults, should we accept it, is to observe everyday life and define internal needs, even though we may have no experience with having been fed by our parents. For instance, did your parents feed your need for the *warmth of understanding* as provided by their ability to acknowledge your strengths and weaknesses with empathy and compassion, rather than the judgment of approval or disapproval?

In addition, did your parents acknowledge the *reality* of death, and then discuss the *meaning* of death in terms of defining *conscious life purposes*? Or did your parents share their *response* to the reality of death, as well as their purposes apart from religious beliefs or philosophical ideas? Did your parents ever discuss internal needs on any level? Or did they define the internal potentials unique to human beings? Or did you ever have a discussion about what, if anything, is necessary to make human life satisfying and meaningful?

Note that each question and topic requires conscious experience, specific insights, and a detailed understanding. In normal life, our education is vague, general, and full of simplistic generalizations: like the popular belief that because someone is pretty, handsome, rich, makes us laugh, or shows us a good time; that these are reasonable criteria for signing-up for the lifetime association we call marriage.

If you observe that lifespan puts a limit on your time to be alive, and that death can happen anytime, then you will also see these facts create a *need* to adopt *conscious purposes* for everyday life that will lead to satisfaction and meaning. Once you see a need for conscious purposes, you can explore this need by first observing ordinary people, and then by reading biographies of famous people, alive and dead, to learn what, if anything, will make human life meaningful. As you learn, you can begin to select your life's purposes, and at the same time, acquire the real-life experience necessary to help a child define his/her conscious life's purposes.

Next, you can learn to observe your own strengths and weaknesses with a desire to see yourself accurately, so you can appreciate what you do well, and improve your skill and awareness where improvement will enhance the degree of satisfaction and meaning you experience in everyday life. As you learn to acknowledge yourself, you will also learn to acknowledge a child without judgment, but with accurate and compassionate observations. You will also learn how to help a child appreciate his/her talents and strengths, and improve on weaknesses because you have done this for yourself. You will never again hide behind the old cliché, "Do as I say, not as I do!"

Can you now see that feeding internal needs by accurately acknowledging strengths and weaknesses, exploring significant life topics, and sharing your responses to being alive are *personal* experiences necessary to provide warmth and understanding, and to *educate by modeling*, not *preaching?*

Innocent Sensual Experience

Children are born curious and instinctively want to connect with reality thru innocent sensual experience. This is one reason babies and toddlers want to put everything they can reach into their mouths, and are often avidly interested in all the fascinating sights, sounds, and textures that for them is an infinitely diverse sensual world where every new thing is to be seen, touched, tasted, and explored.

A normal education reduces or extinguishes a child's innocent sensuality by slowly replacing it with ideas of good, bad, right and wrong. We also replace a child's curiosity and questions with all the normal assumptions and answers about life, love, family, culture, country, religion, politics, economics, wisdom, nature, beauty and truth. No significant internal topic is left open for exploration and discovery.

The infusion of normal ideas and beliefs into our young brains redirects our efforts from *sensually exploring the world* to *accumulating socially acceptable pictures* of what life and the world offer, and how we should respond. Once redirected, we are soon taught that Nature was created by God and filled with abundant resources solely for the *pleasure and comfort* of human beings. Until very recently there has been no understanding that the Earth's resources are limited, while human reproductive capacity seems infinite, nor have we understood that along with the technology to destroy or nurture the *external* world of planet Earth comes the *internal* responsibility to protect and preserve Mother Nature.

The idea that the Earth's resources were planted here by God for human beings to exploit has been around for thousands of years, but has become particularly dangerous now because our population has increased so insanely fast, and our resources are diminishing like water off a mountaintop. If we humans become *observation-based,* and apply the obvious math, we would *see* that an infinitely expanding population in a finite space is not just *probable,* but *certain* disaster.

Then if we connected to reality through innocent sensual experience we would truly *care about* protecting Nature because we need her not only for *external* existence, but also for the *internal* experience of beauty, wonder, adventure and inspiration. A complete understanding of the crucial role Nature plays in our external existence and internal fulfillment would create the desire and will necessary to curb exploitation in favor of preserving and protecting the source of our personal and collective well-being and continued existence.

Without changing from normal to conscious education, or from the normal idea, belief, and feeling-based *reaction* to being alive to an observation-based and innocently sensual *experience* of being alive, then each generation of human beings will continue to exploit the Earth's resources to the full extent of their capacity, and certain disaster for the majority will be the inevitable outcome.

This is the *big picture* I include to help create a burning desire for a conscious education. The *little picture* is that a conscious education is necessary for all internal fulfillment, to create meaning, understand love, and to become wise.

When we cultivate our children's ability to experience innocent sensual experience, then we teach them by example to make space in their lives for the experience of beauty in Nature, music, art, books, movies, or a significant truth succinctly and artfully expressed. We also teach children to see beauty in innocence, authenticity, creativity, and conscious intelligence applied with whole-hearted caring.

With a *normal* education we tend to see beauty as just another commodity to be exploited for profit, or to provide stimulation, excitement, or pleasure. With a *conscious* education we see that we *need* beauty as a life-affirming source of energy and inspiration, as well as a connection to a sensual experience of being alive that keeps us grounded in reality and internally capable of love and wisdom.

When the exploitive attitudes and practices of the now *legally human* inter-national corporate presence successfully completes their purpose to commercialize every last corner of all human minds and emotions, as well as planet Earth — beauty, truth, love and wisdom now endangered, will finally become extinct, soon to be followed by the whole species, and whoever is still around to experience this tragic end — probably won't mind! The reason we won't mind is that everything that makes life worth living will disappear first, so when human life itself disappears there will be little loss.

We see this process in the big picture of all human life, and in the little picture of each individual existence. When a Nelson Mandela or Abraham Lincoln dies, the whole world mourns — but when we lose a J.P. Morgan or Steve Jobs no one really cares — why? Nelson Mandela and Abraham Lincoln brought models of integrity, caring, and the willingness to suffer for a life-affirming purpose into an otherwise jaded and exploitive world, and we love them for their example, and the fact they give us hope we can all grow and improve.

On the other hand, J.P. Morgan and Steve Jobs cared only about their egos and advantages, did their best to control every pain and pleasure, and never did understand or care about learning how to be loving and wise, so their existences were commercially successful, but personally impoverished.

The same choice is offered to you and me, only in a smaller and more anonymous arena. The question for everyone is which example would you rather follow — and why? Remember Hatherley's law — Purpose Determines Outcome!

Exploring and Discovering

Should you want to follow the examples set by Mandela and Lincoln, as well as by Jesus, Buddha, Gandhi, Martin Luther King, etc., then acquiring a *conscious internal education* is the path. If you want to follow the road of J.P and Steve, you don't have to do anything, your *normal education* provides preparation enough for that outcome.

Of course, a normal education does not guarantee you will be as externally successful as J.P. and Steve. For that degree of success, you must have clearly defined purposes, an intensely focused mind and emotions, ruthlessness, luck, and of course, an innate drive and commercial intelligence.

Assuming you would like to continue with a conscious education, nothing is more critical than mastering the ability to *explore* the facts of each new situation and *discover* what is true. It is this process of exploring and discovering that created modern science, which in turn spawned the monster force called technology that is now shaping everyone's life. While technology has provided mixed blessings, the insights that accumulate into wisdom have no downside. Nor do the insights used to understand the experience and expression of real love have a downside.

The purpose for *exploring and discovering* what is true and needed for ourselves, life, and other people is to acquire the *living insights* that we need to understand and integrate the experience of love and wisdom into everyday experience. I say *living insights* because we do not use our insight to create dead end theories, ideas, or beliefs about love or wisdom, but *working hypotheses* that we test against actual experience, so our understanding, skill, and mastery constantly expand as the breadth and depth of our insight grows and changes.

For instance, understanding precisely what is required to create *human happiness* has been an extremely critical topic that no one has yet been able to define in enough detail to have an observable and life-affirming effect on the majority of human beings. What we need now is apply the process of exploring and discovering to accumulate insight into this critical topic, test our insight against actual experience, and then see if we develop the *wisdom* to make a life-affirming difference in the everyday experience of ordinary people.

<u>Understanding Human Happiness</u>

Normal education does offer a vision of what is needed for human happiness. In the normal view, happiness is defined almost entirely by the desire to acquire control over security and approval, and enough wealth for a comfortable and pleasant existence. Of course, the normal view also includes the idea that we can never have *too much* security, approval, or wealth, so more is always considered better.

In the normal view, developing love is seen as a feeling that mysteriously shows up when we find the right person, or a child is born. Wisdom, on the other hand, is assumed to be a natural consequence of experience and aging. Neither love nor wisdom is seen as requiring special attention or training to develop. In fact, the new-age fantasy is that we have love and wisdom lurking around inside us just waiting to make their presence known. Ah, if only it was true!

It is also part of the normal vision of life to assume that *internal* needs and potentials feed and fulfill themselves, as long as we get the *external* under control. As a result, for a person with a normal education there is no reason to explore *internal* motivations, purposes, needs or potentials in detail. Consequently, a normal person is largely oblivious of their internal experience, and sees no problem with this fact.

With a *conscious education,* we soon observe that we need enough *external* wealth to survive, and *internal development* to create the lasting satisfaction and permanent meaning necessary to create a genuine and complete human happiness.

By observing ordinary experience, we see that some satisfactions create a lasting contentment, and others are momentary and leave in their wake no trace they ever existed. It is common for people who define a good life as a continuous experience of fine food, travel, shopping, sports, and partying (young folks term), or visiting (old folks word) with friends to discover **after** they get everything they wanted that it meant nothing, so they feel empty inside and wonder, "Is this all there is?"

The eventual disenchantment with the normal concept of happiness is so common, anyone who wants to observe can quickly see it. Once we see that pleasure does not create happiness, the obvious question is: "What does?" We can start by observing Nature and seeing that animals are happy when they are free to fulfill their potentials, and unhappy when caged-up. Even when their external needs are amply fed, if animals are unable to fulfill their potentials they are bored and unhappy. There is a lesson here for you and me.

The lesson is that we need to first identify and define every internal and external need and potential, and then we must master each and every one. Following this process will result in the experience of lasting satisfaction and permanent meaning necessary for a level of enduring happiness rarely seen in the largely unhappy story of human civilization.

Human beings are the only animal who have the potential to experience and create beauty, love, and wisdom, so it stands to reason that if we fulfill these internal potentials, we will create a lasting and authentic level of real happiness.

On the other hand, if we fail to fulfill these potentials, we can fully expect to create an equally long-lasting and authentic level of anxiety, discontent, and underlying unhappiness. This is obviously not the whole story of how to understand and create lasting human happiness, but it offers a starting place for acquiring what are in fact many layers and levels of understanding, skill, and mastery.

Building Character

A primary purpose of education is to build character. In the old days the word "character" was commonly used to identify the *internal* strengths and weaknesses that defined a person's response to being alive, and to the responsibilities to himself, family, social institutions, culture, and the well-being of the human species. As a result, someone who was competent in his profession, warm and caring with his family, honest in his business dealings with other people, and responsible toward his social and political duties toward community and country was seen as being of *good character.*

Actually, if we *experientially* understood and fulfilled this traditional view of character, our lives would be improved. In modern times, what do you see defines the *character* of normal people. Is integrity, consciousness, caring, and a sophisticated degree of internal competence normal? Or do you see that self-absorption, a desire to control pleasantness and security, a lack of self-worth, chronic anxiety, and a reluctance to be responsible for mistakes more the norm?

Once again, education is the key. With normal education we create a normal character that is defined by a lack of emotional security and self-worth, unaware of internal needs and potentials, self-absorbed to the max, and determined to avoid responsibility for personal inadequacies, mistakes, or causing other people pain. In other words, what in the old days people referred to as possessing low, or poor character.

By contrast, if we provide a conscious education for ourselves and our children, then we will create a new normal where integrity, consciousness, caring, internal and external competence, and the willingness to work and suffer for life-affirming purposes is *normal*. One consequence will be that satisfying and intimate emotional bonds will be common rather than rare, as will personal fulfillment and the internal competence to nurture ourselves, children, other people and planet Earth, which of course, benefits everyone.

Part II

Developmental Tasks

of Adolescence

A Historical Perspective

What, if anything, is necessary to make you and me fully human in the *internal* sense of the word? We all know what makes us human in the *external* sense, but has anyone ever clearly defined precisely what is required to make you and me *internally human*? I have studied the traditional intellectual and psychological pursuits and seen that some famous people have identified love and wisdom as being critical to being fully human, but even then, I have never run across anyone who has defined either love or wisdom in precise *experiential* terms, and then created a *detailed map* for how to fulfill these peculiarly human potentials.

What about you? Have you ever run across anyone, living or dead, who has provided precise *experiential* definitions of love and wisdom, or truth and beauty, and then created maps for how to fulfill these potentials? If you have, be sure to let me know. If you haven't, then maybe we can agree that while most people acknowledge that *love, truth, beauty and wisdom* are important potentials, we have yet to meet anyone who has experientially defined even one potential, and no one who has created detailed maps so we can fulfill all four potentials and integrate them into everyday life.

What this means, if it is true, is that homo sapiens (our species) has existed for two hundred thousand years and still cannot define what is required to be internally human.

On the one hand, this news is a bit depressing, but on the other, now that I have defined precisely how to become *internally* fully human, we have a choice, you and me. With clear definitions and detailed maps we can master the skills and awareness necessary to define and express love, experience and create beauty, and finally, by pursuing truth we can accumulate an *inventory of insight* that first develops into understanding, and then over time, grows into real wisdom.

In our human past, essentially for the first one hundred and ninety thousand years, we were hunters and gatherers, lived literally hand to mouth, had very short life spans, and all that separated us from other animals was an opposable thumb and the fact we liked to leave graffiti on the walls of caves. If we think about it, leaving graffiti (my word, not the technical term), was motivated in part by an *internal* hunger to leave some physical reminder that we were here, and to preserve some small piece of our experience for the future.

Animals do not experience a hunger, or *need for meaning*, so this need sets people apart from animals. The problem is that most people never define even the first step toward feeding their hunger for meaning. It also true that people suffer internal damage when this *instinctual* need is neither acknowledged nor fed. I say this need is *instinctual* because humans have an innate potential for self-awareness, which brings with it an internal hunger for a meaningful life.

If any animal (including humans), has little or no self-awareness, then he will experience little or no hunger for a meaningful life. Instead, survival will be the first concern, but no matter how *successful at surviving* an individual may be – death, and with it personal extinction – is the inevitable outcome. For most of human history, including up to present day, people have lived like other animals and tried to insure personal survival for as long as possible. Only a few humans, perhaps including the ancient graffiti artists, had enough self-awareness to open the door to the strongest of all fully human internal longings, greater even than our universal hunger for love, and that is the desire for our lives to acquire some level of real and lasting meaning.

Even as a young man, Abraham Lincoln was consciously aware that he wanted to contribute something that would make a long-term and life-affirming difference for people. Anne Frank, when only 14, wrote in her diary that she would never be content to be "just a wife and mother" and to leave in her life's wake a completely anonymous existence. Instead, she wanted to "live on beyond my death" through what she wrote. Both Lincoln and Anne Frank wanted to contribute, and thru their contributions feed their internal hunger for creating a meaningful life.

Today, everyone seems to agree that a *secure and pleasant* life is the highest goal, and you rarely hear anyone mention a hunger for meaning, or if they do it is as a whiny lament rather than to *explore* this important topic and *discover* what is true and needed. If you feel a hunger for the *meaning* created by learning how to *express love, pursue truth, experience beauty and develop wisdom*, then you have a real reason to understand and complete all your developmental tasks.

Observing Vs. Believing & Feeling

Everyone knows that human history has often been defined by patterns of conflict over power, wealth, religious, political, and economic beliefs, resources, women, land, and even hurt feelings that we like to disguise as *matters of honor!* In all the predictable conflicts we can see *patterns of purposes and process* that will help us understand the lack of internal development in human beings across the entire spectrum of time that we refer to as *civilization*.

In pre-civilized time human *purposes* were to survive and procreate, and the *process* we relied on was observation. It is important to note that pre-civilized people must rely on *observing* the facts of nature in order to survive. By contrast, with civilization comes the ability to store food and accumulate wealth, so we can afford the luxury of relying on beliefs and feelings, as well as create neurotic fears and fantasies, and still survive.

Pre-civilized people, on the other hand, have to understand nature in order to survive, which requires relying on *observations* to get the facts, and *reason* to determine what is true and needed. In primitive conditions people can rely on beliefs and feelings only to explain non-essential realities like the source of life, death, sickness, growth and decay in terms of superstitious beliefs, feelings and fantasies. Much the same as we still do today. The primary difference now is that we also feel entitled to control pleasantness, acquire security, and spend as much time as we can being entertained.

With civilization we enjoy longer lives and more securi-ty, and along with these improvements is the opportunity to experience boredom. Pre-civilized life was so short, difficult, and dangerous there was little time to be bored. Civilization changed all that. Nowadays, people *believe* that happiness is defined by power and pleasure, and more is always better. Rather than just surviving and procreating, we want leisure, luxury, and the feeling of power that comes from acquiring enough wealth to follow every impulse and get other people to serve our desires. Becoming free to live our lives based on *beliefs* rather than *observations* was an unexpected luxury of civilization, and today nearly everyone indulges that luxury.

From the simplistic belief that happiness requires power and pleasure, and there is no such thing as having too much, almost all human conflict has been created. Wars, greed, ex-ploiting other people and the planet, all prejudice from racial to religious, from gender bias to cultural conflict, political and economic manipulation, you name it, this belief helped to create it. This simplistic belief has been a primary source for creating irresolvable divisions between countries, races, genders, religions, and even between family members.

One of Hatherley's little known *principles of life* says that **"If you can't identify the source of a problem, you can't fix it!"** I now suggest that one critical source of the world's problems is a lack of internal development, and one reason for this species-wide inadequacy is the *belief* that happiness requires power and pleasure, and that *control* of security, pain, and pleasure is both possible and necessary.

Dr. Paul Hatherley

Understanding Vs. Control

By studying human history from a developmental pers-pective we see that homo sapiens began existence confined to an *observation-based response to being alive,* in part because it was necessary for survival. Then, after about one hundred and ninety five thousand years, we stumbled onto civiliza-tion and discovered that we could rely on *beliefs and feelings* to explain the mystery of being alive, and to escape painful realities. We also learned that we could use beliefs to ac-quire the *illusion of control,* not only over our own perception of reality, but also that of other people.

For instance, every time we exploit, enslave, take advan-tage, or destroy another person or whole class of persons, part of the process is to convince ourselves, and if possible the damaged party or parties, that we are superior. Hence, one reason slavery in the United States lasted for a whop-ping two hundred years was because white enslavers truly convinced themselves, and to a much lesser degree even the African-American slaves, that white people were superior.

For more than two centuries this cruel institution was supported by Christian churches in the South, and justified by characterizing African-Americans as being inferior, not really human, and put here by God, like all Nature's bounty, for white people to exploit. It is important to notice that pre-judice is always *belief-based — prejudice cannot be supported by an observation-based understanding of reality.*

It wasn't just African-Americans who were exploited

and considered inferior. Women were not allowed to vote until the third decade of the 20th century because the wise founding fathers of the grand experiment in freedom called the United States of America thought they too, were inferior. Think about it, for all but the last ninety or so of the two hundred thousand years of human existence women everywhere have been treated as the property of men, denied the opportunity to fulfill themselves, and often brutally treated with no legal recourse whatsoever. In 19th century England a man could legally beat his wife as long as he used a stick no bigger than his wrist. How enlightened!

Also, the Catholic Church, a bastion of Christ's love and compassion, instituted three hundred years of the *inquisition* where torture and burning at the stake, a horrible death, was common for no offense worse than not *believing*, or simply being accused of being a witch. How is it that no one I have read has even tried to understand these institutionalized human cruelties in psychological, or developmental terms?

Is it perhaps because as a group we still retain the seeds, or source of these abuses by being belief and feeling-based, and fail to become *observation-based* so we rely on questions, reason and experiment to create a true understanding of life, ourselves, and other people? If anyone needs proof of ongoing human cruelty, the 20th century provided plenty. The examples of mass cruelty in this century by Germany, Japan, Russia, China and the United States (for instance the millions of North Vietnamese killed with carpet bombing) not to mention the genocide in various African countries.

One consequence of internal development is that people will be *observation-based*, will want the *meaning* provided by *understanding*, will develop a *conscious connection* to ordinary experience, and *empathy and compassion* for other people. In the process, people will learn that feeding needs and fulfilling potentials creates happiness, not power or pleasure, so their primary priority will be to master the four internal human potentials of expressing love, pursuing truth, experiencing and creating beauty, and developing wisdom.

The purpose of this chapter is to enlarge understanding of the purpose and meaning behind internal development. We all need internal development for personal fulfillment, as well as to genuinely love our mates, children, friends, and fellow human beings. In addition, it is critical to the survival of our species, and essential for human happiness that we develop our minds and emotions until we fulfill every part of our potential to become fully conscious, whole-hearted in our caring, and competent to understand and nurture ourselves and other people.

To confirm or reject this last statement, I suggest you observe everyday experience to see what is true. I also encourage you to read my other books to get different angles and details on life's critical subjects, and then read or listen to people who are observation-based and care about life and nature, and discover for yourself the political, economic, and environmental facts that define the world you and I live in, and perhaps you will see we are in grave danger, and that the biggest danger is our own lack of internal development.

Understanding Adolescence

Childhood can be seen as taking up the first twelve years of life. Adolescence begins at age thirteen and continues until age nineteen or twenty. Adulthood defines the rest of existence and contains layer upon layer of developmental tasks and stages that provide daunting new challenges and opportunities for growth and change in each new decade. That being said, not all developmental stages are created equal, and adolescence easily takes the prize for being the most intense and challenging.

Most people will agree with the truth in this statement, especially parents, based only on personal experience and a cursory look at the facts. In the Foreword, I described life as *"ceaseless motion in a context of unrelenting change"* and adolescence fits this definition, only on steroids! Every *external* and *internal* thing is changing in adolescence: our bodies, minds, emotions, responsibilities, roles, demands and choices, and through it all we have no training in how to handle any of it.

Instead, each generation is expected to *somehow muddle thru,* and muddle thru we do. The problem with muddling is that we have no information or competence. This means we are clueless as to what we are doing, what motivates us, what our purposes are, or what we need. Instead, we just react to daily events and feelings trying to get through intact, while trying to feel as good as we can about ourselves.

In spite of the fact that every generation from time memorial has gone thru the same painful trials and tribulations, we still have no definitions or maps for how to successfully identify and complete our adolescent developmental tasks. The sad consequence is that few people complete this stage of development. The only unknown is how much damage will we cause by not understanding our internal needs and potentials, our inability to provide emotional warmth and build emotional bonds, and our lack of competence to create satisfaction and meaning in our professional lives?

What do you see was your experience with adolescence? Did you get help in identifying with your gender, understanding your role in being masculine or feminine, or seeing yourself accurately and choosing a career based on your talents and preferences with an eye to lasting satisfaction — not just security, approval or money? Or, were you taught how to clearly define the conscious purposes necessary to create meaning, or how to feed and fulfill the internal needs and potentials necessary to build true personal fulfillment? Finally, did anyone help you experientially define warm and cold, personal and impersonal, or needs and wants, so you were internally prepared to create intimacy and consciously competent to build lasting emotional bonds?

If you received specific training for any of the developmental tasks listed above, then you are a lucky duck! Most people, including the author, do not. Careful observation of friends, family, and people in the world around us quickly confirms that *muddling through* with some damage is normal.

Adolescence Builds on Childhood

One huge problem with adolescent developmental tasks is that to successfully complete them we must first have successfully completed our childhood tasks. Given what you have read and learned so far, how does this pre-requisite strike you? Rather daunting, you say? I agree, it is daunting. Nonetheless it is reality, so let's get on with understanding how to tackle our tasks and complete them, daunting or not.

The biggest problem with adolescent tasks is they are complicated and many, so we desperately need to master the basics necessary to *explore* reality and *discover* what is true. This childhood task requires that we learn from our parents, or teach ourselves how to preserve our natural instinct to be innocently curious, and then develop that instinct by becoming *observation-based* rather than *belief and feeling-based*.

Most children learn from both parents and culture to value the *illusion of control* over the *reality of understanding*, and what everyone most often wants to control are feelings. This desire dooms most adolescents to a stormy, conflicted, and painful developmental stage where they muddle thru doing the best they can, but stumble into adulthood having failed to even define and understand their adolescent tasks, much less successfully complete them.

Everyone knows that adolescence is a time of feelings that are largely *out of control*, and what most people *believe* is that a teenager's task is to get their feelings under control. I have never met an adolescent or parent who truly wanted to *understand* the hungers, conflicts, and developmental tasks of this transitional stage of life unless it brought *control* with it.

If a child is raised by parents who help him *explore* ordinary experience, so he learns how to *discover* what is true, then by the time he enters adolescence he will see that *understanding* is a necessary pre-requisite to learn from experience. With this early training, an adolescent can acquire the skills and awareness necessary to feed needs, fulfill potentials, and complete his developmental tasks.

On the other hand, when a child is raised with the normal purpose of trying to control every negative by avoiding, denying, or explaining it away, and has failed to complete the childhood tasks for emotional safety and self-worth, then his negative feelings are guaranteed to be *out of control*, and the only thing he will want in adolescence is to make them go-away, so he can get them *under control*. This is one of the few things teen-agers and their parents frequently agree on!

The most popular ways for teen-agers to *control* negative feelings is to use drugs and/or alcohol, party with friends, anxiously pursue approval, or rebelliously try to prove they don't care. Of course, stormy relationships with the opposite sex are also a common source for both comfort and turmoil. This is because adolescence is a time when raging hormones combine with chronic unsatisfied hungers for emotional warmth and real understanding, and these forces erupt into desperately intense relationships. While parents and teen-agers may agree on wanting to get these feelings *under control*, they often disagree on the preferred method!

Understanding Adolescent Tasks

We have seen that one source of a tragic adolescence is we enter it handicapped by failing to complete childhood tasks, so early neurotic patterns become even more twisted by responsibilities and developmental tasks we are totally unprepared to explore and understand. For instance, as adolescents we need to *identify with our gender*, which means in part that we need to define masculine and feminine traits, and integrate both, so we are *internally* complete.

This means we need to learn that one critical characteristic of being feminine is to be *receptive*, and a primary feature of being masculine is to be *masterful*, and to be *internally complete* a person must be able to define and integrate both. Often, adolescents are confused about their gender roles in terms of *how* to be masculine or feminine, and training with detailed definitions would go a long way toward relieving their anxiety and replacing it with a specific plan for how to be both receptive and masterful in everyday life.

In being *receptive* we learn how to observe and take-in painful **and** pleasant feelings and experiences. Acquiring this skill requires we become *consciously vulnerable*, which needs to be backed-up by a *conscious purpose* to learn about needs and potentials, as well as life, ourselves, and other people. With the insight and understanding we acquire by being *receptive*, we are prepared to develop the skill and awareness necessary to *master* internal needs and potentials, as well as understand and nurture other people and nature.

In the process of learning to be receptive and masterful, we acquire the understanding and competence we need to tackle all the other complex tasks of ordinary adolescence. (BTW, there are many ways I could explain this process, but in the moment this seems to be the easiest.) If you want to understand all the developmental tasks for yourself, picture in your mind's eye the facts that define a child's life, then picture the facts that define an adolescent's life. Now compare the two pictures to see what is similar and different.

With this assignment, I am asking that you start training your mind to view life, yourself, and other people thru mental pictures rather than concepts. Pictures contain more information and are more fluid and flexible than concepts. As you picture the facts of a child or adolescent's life keep in mind their lives are defined by three universal categories: *personal, relationship, and profession.* For children and adolescents, profession is defined by being in school. Of course, for adults profession is defined by how we earn a living.

For children, life is defined by attending school, playing alone or with other children, and minimal external responsibilities like brushing their teeth and cleaning their room — when mom or dad can get them to do it! Even these tasks can be anxiety producing if children do not feel emotionally safe, or lack self-worth. For instance, even if a child does well in school, without self-worth he often feels anxious he can never do well-enough, or won't continue to do well.

Even playing can be anxiety producing if a child feels insecure in his value and anxious about being accepted by other children, or insecure in his/her ability to relate to other children. Sometimes, a deep insecurity will motivate a child to become a bully, so he can prove his superiority. This trait can easily be carried thru adolescence and into adulthood.

With these *pictures of childhood*, can you see that to be internally healthy children need emotional safety, self-worth, and an accurate self-awareness, as well as the competence to *explore* ordinary experience with the purpose of *discovering* what is true for themselves, other people, and nature? These universal needs define the developmental tasks of children, and are easily seen by parents trained to observe.

Now, we can picture the facts that define an adolescent's life and contrast them with children. For instance, as children we are constantly growing physically and becoming more coordinated and mobile, and mentally more able to understand complex topics like time, math, and meaning.

By the end of adolescence, we *top-out* in physical growth, and due to puberty we also experience other changes and become sexually mature beings capable of reproduction. Now we are faced with needing to learn how to relate to the opposite sex and define ourselves, not just in terms of gender, but in terms of our character, or what kind of man or woman we want to be, and in terms of the career we choose.

In all three areas, personal, relationships, and profession, we are faced with having to define the multiple roles and purposes necessary to build a satisfying and meaningful life. Of course, if we have no clue as to what we need, or what is required to create a satisfying and meaningful life, then we have tasks that exceed our developmental capacity, which in turn can create unbearable stress and anxiety.

Can you now see that with all the tasks and choices that accompany adolescence, if we are still struggling with self-worth and emotional safety, and we have a distorted self-awareness with no ability to explore life and discover what is true, then adolescent tasks can become not just difficult, but impossible?

We need the clarity and confidence that comes from completing our childhood tasks of mastering emotional safety, self-worth, an accurate self-awareness, and the ability to explore and discover to be developmentally competent to handle the changes and choices of adolescence. Without this fundamental competence, adolescent developmental tasks create what is often a lifetime of confusion, conflict, distortion and discontent.

Parenting Adolescents

As every parent of a teenager knows first-hand, parenting adolescents is not for the faint-of-heart! On the one hand, if parents have completed their own developmental tasks, and are trained to first help their child, and in time their adolescent complete his tasks, then adolescence can be a joyful time of *exploring, discovering, sharing and growing* that creates satisfying and meaningful emotional bonds for everyone.

On the other hand, when parents fail to complete their own developmental tasks, and their children become adolescents with inadequate emotional safety and self-worth, there is hell to pay, and parenting adolescents can be anything from mildly to severely difficult, or even totally impossible. As many a parent knows, a teenager on an emotional or acting-out rampage can make life an ongoing nightmare. Two very different scenarios for the same developmental stage.

If you would prefer the former as compared to the latter scenario, then it is time to define your personal response to being alive. Have you responded to having a mind, body, emotions and life span by relying on *beliefs and feelings* for the *purpose* of *controlling a pleasant life*, or have you adopted an *observation-based* response for the *purpose of understanding* yourself, life, and other people?

You probably think this is an odd place to begin. The problem is that with a normal feeling/belief/control-based response to being alive it is impossible to help our children grow-up to be internally complete human beings. In fact, when our response to being alive is to adopt a normal desire for *controlled pleasantness*, the extent of caring for our children is often limited to wanting them to do well externally, and to not become a chronic problem, or bother.

In the mind of a *belief/feeling/control-based* parent, as long as our children are silent, we fail to notice or don't care that they suffer from chronic anxiety, low self-worth, a painfully distorted self-image, or from being constantly hungry for internal fulfillments they can neither define nor provide. In stark contrast, an *observation/understanding-based* parent consciously notices and truly cares about their child's external *and* internal well-being, and consciously develops the competence to nurture both dimensions of their children's needs.

Since becoming *observation/understanding-based* requires focused effort and the willingness to suffer while learning, it is not a popular option. Instead, parents want to send their children to experts where a new technique, or just someone else can be responsible for *fixing the child,* and the parent's role is often restricted to throwing money at the problem.

Taking a *fix the child* approach, rather than helping them complete their developmental tasks is normal, but largely ineffective. Even if the child is brought *under control*, he will still never understand internal fulfillment, the process of emotional bonding, or learn how to *express love, pursue truth, experience beauty or develop wisdom*. These experiences are a direct consequence of completing developmental tasks.

First Steps

The first step in consciously connecting with anyone—a child, adolescent, or adult—is to master expressing genuine and whole-hearted interest in *understanding* his *perspective:* that is, his needs, wants, motivations, purposes, thoughts, feelings, response to being alive and significant experiences. This requires not only sincere interest, but also practice before we learn to keep our attention focused so we ask innocent and intelligent questions, remember the answers, ask more questions, and become competent to articulate another person's perspective until he/she feels understood.

A conscious connection established thru the process of providing interest that leads to understanding is the most basic and effective way to communicate emotional warmth. Everyone on the planet is hungry for emotional warmth, and that goes triple for adolescents experiencing overwhelming internal and external changes without the benefit of having completed their childhood tasks.

Understanding is difficult to value or provide when we have spent our lives trying to control outcomes, and all we care about is avoiding pain and solving problems. By contrast, in the pursuit of understanding we explore another person's issues until we see the causes and consequences in specific and sometimes excruciating detail. When we *explore* a topic we never know what we will find. Some problems can be understood, fixed and resolved, while others can be understood and shared, but not resolved.

The willingness to explore a child's pain, even when we are the major source of creating it, takes courage, skill, and real caring. Committing the effort to develop all three proves to a child that we genuinely love them, and also that we are in turn, worth being loved. I know it is not *politically correct* to suggest, even though we all intuitively know it is true, but being lovable requires that we develop character traits that create life-affirming purposes, priorities, caring, skills, and courage that all together make us *worthy of respect and love.*

Providing emotional warmth requires that we master new purposes and priorities, as well as new levels of skill, caring and courage. This degree of change cannot happen without focused attention, specific training, and conscious effort. That's the bad news, the good news is that once we learn how to provide emotional warmth this skill is effective in creating intimacy and emotional bonds in every relation-ship—parent/child, romantic, friends, business associates, and even for turning strangers into friends.

To understand an adolescent's internal pain we must ob-serve that all emotional pain is caused by some internal need that often goes unrecognized, and is certainly not fed. The typical adolescent pains include but are not limited to feel-ing lonely, (in part from not being understood) issues with self-worth, inadequate to connect with the opposite sex, an-xious about academic or athletic performance, and free-floating feelings of anger, confusion, or chronic discontent he may act-out by hurting himself, or by harshly judging and being critical of other people.

Parents have no hope of understanding an adolescent's pain unless they understand the internal need that caused it. With the normal lack of training to be either a whole person or competent parent, the typical situation is that parent's ignore their children's internal pain until the degree of acting-out is so extreme they are forced to acknowledge it, and then they take a "let's fix it" stance, which means they give advice, lecture, or send the adolescent to a counselor or therapist.

What parents usually do not even consider is learning how to define and feed the internal needs that cause the pain. This is to be expected because there is no training in our culture for how to identify and feed internal needs. *What are an adolescent's internal needs? First is the need for emotional warmth that as we have seen is expressed in part through whole-hearted interest and a patient exploring of the child's experience until we truly understand him/her.*

Next, if we review our list of typical adolescent pains, we can see the need to help an adolescent first understand himself, and then learn how to make meaningful internal connections with friends and the opposite sex. This requires in part that we be competent to use conversation to explore another person's experience and perspective, so we can teach our children through both example and education how to create satisfying emotional connections with other people.

Of course, if as parents we have not mastered the ability to use conversation to create meaningful connections and deep emotional bonds, we will not be competent to teach anyone else. This is frequently the crux of the problem.

"Lead, Follow, or Get Out of the Way!"

This line was made famous by Lee Iacocca when he was CEO of Chrysler and made an advertisement challenging the other car companies. I am using it here because in the tricky business of helping adolescents master their developmental tasks parents must be flexible and acquire the competence to know how and when to: *"Lead, follow, or get out of the way!"* At different times and in unexpected ways all three modes of responding are needed.

For instance, if we want to understand an adolescent's pain and failure, or joy and success, we need to be competent to *follow*, so we can *explore* their experience and *discover* how to share in it—whether painful or pleasant. At other times, when the adolescent has a well-defined purpose, or is experimenting in a life-affirming way with learning about himself, life, or other people, it may be our job as parents to just *get out of the way,* so he/she can learn on their own.

The most difficult job for parents is to learn how to *lead* an adolescent into understanding the many choices he must make during this period of life. The reason for the difficulty is that when they were adolescents, most parents made their choices by *unconsciously reacting* to circumstances and never did understand the options, and still don't. This often results in making critical life choices that are less than satisfying and meaningful, and sometimes, permanently painful.

To understand an adolescent's choices and dilemmas requires we learn about our own, and this requires real love.

Universal Adolescent Choices

As everyone knows, adolescence is life's quintessential *time of transition*. In this phase, we are making the transition from being a child, whose main job is to attend school and play, to becoming an adult with the responsibility of being competent to fend for ourselves and master every internal and external need and potential in three large categories: *personal life, significant relationships, and profession*. We must grow from barely a hint of responsibility to being accountable for everything in a very short period of time, and as the world becomes more complex, impersonal and intimidating, adolescence grows in difficulty and significance.

To help an adolescent make life-affirming choices, parents must understand life's options, which usually requires exploring issues the parent *unconsciously reacted* to in their adolescence. Now, the parent must mentally revisit the adolescent experience until they *understand* the developmental tasks and can help their adolescent *consciously respond* rather than *unconsciously react*. This internal education will enable the adolescent to make life-affirming choices based on their unique talents and preferences. Easier said than done!

What are life's options? We can start by acknowledging the basic facts: that is, we are all born with a mind, body, emotions and life span. Next, we see that our potential for becoming self-aware enough to understand ourselves, other people, and nature is unique in the animal kingdom. So the first choice is: "How do we want to respond to being alive?"

I first tackled the question of how to respond to the mystery of being alive when at age five when my grandmother died. My parents had dropped me off at grandma's every Monday morning and picked me up every Friday night from age two to four. The reason for this arrangement is that my mother had a part-time job at the city library, which in her mind made taking care of me too much of a burden, while grandma was a stay-at-home grandma who had raised four daughters and was delighted to care for a precocious little boy. In other words, she liked me and my parents didn't.

At age four, after talking early and being quite articulate, I started stuttering, so my mother took me to a psychologist, a surprisingly enlightened response, who learned of the arrangement and stated plainly it had to stop. My parents had noticed that I was devastated every Monday morning in leaving them, and every Friday evening in leaving grandma. In their minds, I was just being a big baby! In all fairness I agreed, and was humiliated by my show of emotion and determined it was way past time for me to man-up. However, I didn't count on the stutter as being collateral damage.

Anyway, grandma was someone I respected and admired. She had gotten thru the depression, raised four girls, put up with a Neanderthal husband and was still rational, warm, competent, and loved me. In return, I loved her with my whole heart, mind and soul. When she died, however, I was all alone in the world, and I really did have to man-up and face the truth. The truth was that I too would die, so "What, if anything, would make my life meaningful?"

My circumstances and innate character propelled me toward tackling this adolescent task a bit early, but truth be told I have felt a sense of urgency all my life, like I have a destiny full of large tasks but little time, so I need to get on with it. The psychologist watched me interact with other children and noted that when another child wanted a toy that was in my hands I readily gave it up, and she counseled my mother to help me *stand-up for myself* and become more assertive. There was no way the psychologist could know that I did not care about toys, or playing for that matter, so if another child wanted a toy in my hands he was welcome to it. In fact, I wanted him to have it because I didn't care about toys, so if he did, great, it was his! Truth is, I was just hanging-out until I could get on with something meaningful.

The first major exploration of my question about what creates meaning began in the fourth grade at age eight, when I read about thirty-five biographies of famous Americans. It was a set of biographies that I found in the school library, and I read every one with my fateful question in mind. This is where I learned to identify life's options. For instance, I discovered that I could respond to life by becoming an artist, politician, warrior, scholar, craftsman, naturalist, teacher, scientist, doctor, lawyer, athlete or businessman.

I also learned that some famous people chose only one or two of these possibilities, and some mastered many. Thomas Jefferson, for example, chose to master many. He was a scholar, politician, lawyer, architect, farmer, violinist, writer, surveyor, inventor, husband, father and friend.

In observing normal people around me, as opposed to famous people in books, I saw that most people chose to master survival and entertainment, and some had a hobby or two, but it became clear that it is rare for modern people to have a driving ambition to master many of life's options. In making up my own mind, I decided that I preferred to follow Jefferson's example, and also Benjamin Franklin, another over-achiever, rather than my more modern peers.

Understanding life's external options and choosing how we want to spend our time is just one part of a larger task of defining ourselves. Reading many biographies helped me with another part of this big task of self-definition, learning what kind of *internal character* I wanted to develop.

For instance, I discovered that many famous people did not understand how to define and develop their internal life. Jefferson, for example, spent his life inadequate to relate to women, even though women were his closest companions. He also did not learn how to take care of them. His eldest daughter was the closest person to him and when he died he was bankrupt, so she had no money and no home since Monticello and all the slaves had to be sold to pay debts.

Another woman close to Jefferson was Sally Hemings, who was a slave he never freed, but who bore him children. What I learned from this was that a meaningful life requires mastering *external* activities as well as *internal* love and wisdom. I also noted that Jefferson in mastering many external activities was motivated mostly by being insanely intelligent and needing to fill his time, but no larger internal purpose.

This was a key awareness because I could see that a person could master every external activity imaginable and still not have a truly satisfying life. The reason is that without a *unifying internal purpose there is no meaning to external success.* Reading Lou Gehrig's biography brought this lesson home because I saw how much I admired the fact that Gehrig's life was defined more by his integrity, endurance, and caring than by his athletic talent, which was immense. Babe Ruth created an even bigger name and baseball legacy, but Gehrig was the bigger man, and even as a child I knew I wanted to be like Gehrig—not Ruth.

The point is that step by step, I was building a picture of the kind of man I wanted to be, and the life I wanted to create. By the time I was an adolescent, my reading and observations taught me that I wanted to be a man's man and a woman's man, so I defined both! My version of a man's man is a combination of athlete, warrior, craftsman, scientist and mountain man in a context of being fiercely independent. A real man's man would also make tons of money, but somehow I never got around to adding that quality to my list.

A woman's man combines all the qualities of a man's man with the addition of being a sensitive scholar and artist who is intimately connected to *life, beauty, love and wisdom.* A woman's man can listen to a woman's innermost thoughts and feelings and understand her experience as well or better than she understands herself, and can articulate the critical insights that define her internal life, so she sees herself more intimately thru his eyes than she ever could all alone.

We see that a man's man is competent in external life, but a woman's man understands life, and uses his insight to create lasting intimacy and genuine emotional bonds. For me, the *unifying internal purpose* for being both a man's man and a woman's man was to make a real contribution to the collective consciousness and caring of the human species. As an adolescent, this *internal purpose* completed my mental picture of how I wanted to respond to this sometimes wonderful, and sometimes terrifying mystery of just being alive.

The point for parents wanting to lead adolescents, or for anyone trying to define him/herself at any stage of life, is that we need a structure to identify the options and make conscious choices based on our talents and preferences. Reading and observing how other people respond to life, as well as seeing how famous people from the past responded, is a very effective way to identify life's options and their predictable consequences, and then choose what we prefer.

Much of the free-floating anxiety and anger expressed by many adolescents arises directly from intuitively sensing they have no picture of what will make life satisfying and meaningful. Instead, the picture they get from peers, parents, teachers and culture is that the value of a normal life is determined by the degree of external success. Consequently, a modern adolescent hears only an ominous silence whenever he tries to understand the internal dimensions of human life. There is in fact nowhere in American culture where we consciously define internal needs and potentials, or specifically address the problem of how to create a meaningful life.

Expressing Love

Leading an adolescent toward a materially sufficient *and* internally meaningful life requires clearly defined purposes that unite external experience with internal fulfillment. Life's critical and timeless *unifying internal purposes* are found in four activities: *expressing love, pursuing truth, experiencing beauty and developing wisdom.* Note that I call these timeless purposes — *activities* — **not** concepts, philosophies, or feelings.

The reason is that people often like to believe that love, truth, beauty and wisdom are *subjective* ideas, beliefs or vague feelings, rather than *objective* experiences that require specific skills and awareness to be understood and mastered. Love is especially mangled in normal minds when it is seen as being defined by ephemeral and mysterious feelings that drift into and out of our hearts like a capricious coastal fog.

Normally, people have only a *foggy notion* of what real love is, but that does not mean that love is not definable. Instead, real love is easily defined if we explore our everyday experience, books and movies, as well as past and present human events, circumstances, relationships and purposes. It is thru the process of observing, asking questions, using our reason and experimenting that we can explore ordinary life and discover for ourselves precisely what love is, *and is not!*

For instance, a little focused attention will quickly reveal that real love is based on *respect and admiration* for a person, purpose, character trait, plant, animal or landscape, or any activity that enhances our intimate connection to being alive.

In addition to being based on respect and admiration, real love is backed-up by a commitment to offer intensely focused attention, innocent interest, whole-hearted energy, and a desire to learn about, understand, nurture and protect what we love. Without the base of respect and admiration, and being backed up by commitment, love is just an impotent intention, or advantage seeking desire, but has nothing whatever to do with caring, understanding, and nurturing.

Now, let's compare this *experiential* definition of real love with what you can observe is the normal vague and foggy notion. What do you see? Is it obvious that if we define love in *experiential* terms then we can observe the facts and soon determine whether we love someone, or not, and whether or not someone loves us? On the other hand, can you see that if we define love as an ephemeral and mysteriously misty feeling we can never know whether we are loving, or loved?

If you can see this significant reality, then perhaps it will be apparent that we all have a vested interest in keeping the definition of love vague—mainly because as long as our definition is foggy we can believe we are loved, and loving, even if the facts contradict our belief. Following this path, we can avoid being held accountable for our actions, and we can swim along in our own little fantasy worlds of feelings and beliefs unhindered by the facts.

Leading an adolescent to *understanding love* requires we replace foggy notions with clear definitions, romantic beliefs with objective understanding, and well-meaning but impotent intentions with conscious caring and competent actions.

Once we observe that love is an objective experience to be understood and mastered, we can expand the role of love in everyday life. For instance, we normally think of love in terms of a romantic involvement, parents toward children, or in identifying something we want or expect to be pleasurable: like when we "love" a great steak, good movie, new car, or hot body. However, after we *understand real love*, we can lead an adolescent into "loving life" by helping him identify and value those things worth his *respect and admiration*.

This exploration will take us into identifying admirable character traits like *integrity, intelligence, courage, caring, innocence and creativity*. Now we can initiate conversations where we clearly define each character trait and identify the *benefits* of developing each one, as well as the *cost* of doing without.

What conversations do you have with your child, adolescent, or even mate? Do you consciously identify significant topics like defining character traits you respect, admire, and truly love, or do you spend your conversational time on tiresome trivial topics that serve only as an empty pastime, but never enhance your self-life-or other-awareness?

In addition to character traits, we can lead an adolescent toward exploring life's options in terms of understanding his internal needs for self-worth, or an accurate self-awareness, or his internal potential to *understand, care, master, create and contribute*. We can also lead an adolescent to connect loving to feeding needs and fulfilling potentials in himself, and helping other people do the same. Finally, we can help an adolescent learn how to *love* truth, beauty and wisdom.

<u>Pursuing Truth & Developing Wisdom</u>

While it should be self-evident that pursuing truth is an inescapable pre-requisite for developing wisdom, many people like to believe that wisdom is a natural consequence of growing old, therefore no special attention or effort is needed, just hang-out long enough and you too will be wise. Sadly, nothing could be further from the truth. But hey, we would never want a fact to interfere with a favorite fantasy!

The reality is that pursuing truth requires focused effort, conscious purposes, and whole-hearted commitment. With these pre-requisites firmly integrated, developing wisdom becomes a natural consequence. Truth is relatively easy to pursue when we are trained to be observation-based, and we know how to ask questions, apply reason, and experiment with what we learn to discover what is true. *When over time our insights accumulate then we acquire understanding, and when understanding leads to defining universal patterns in ourselves, life and other people, we develop wisdom.*

To lead an adolescent toward truth and wisdom, we must model the behaviors and attitudes that show truth and wisdom are satisfying to experience, and meaningful to master. Most parents reveal thru their purposes and priorities that all they value are success, security, entertainment and controlled pleasantness, so pursuing truth and developing wisdom do not show-up in their minds and emotions, or daily purposes and priorities. With this as their only model, is it any wonder adolescents feel lost, and sometimes angry?

Of course, idealistic adolescents find it easy to criticize parents for shallow purposes and priorities, but if we continue to observe we see most adolescents are soon funneled into being a mirror image of their parents, and the drumbeat of normal mediocrity continues on without skipping a beat. This repetition is tragic for both individuals and the species.

The only remedy is for parents to master an observation-based response to being alive driven by a scientific attitude where they *ask questions, apply reason, and actively experiment* in the conscious pursuit of truth and wisdom. For example, a parent might talk with an adolescent about the differences between a tradesman, craftsman, artist and scholar.

The parent could start by noting that a tradesman could be defined as someone who works for money, as opposed to a craftsman who works for love and money. (These definitions are only meant to help provide contrast.) Both occupations work with their hands, but the *purpose* of the craftsman is to make things functional **and** beautiful, while the tradesman is concerned primarily with making things functional.

As we go up the list, we see artists are more specialized, don't care about functionality, but are concerned primarily with beauty. A scholar may be someone who cares mostly about ideas and theories, or he may want to understand life. After defining the purposes in these types of life options, we could ask our adolescent, "What purposes would you would like to pursue? For instance, do you want to work mostly for money, or love?" Working for money is a reasonable response, but is it our adolescent's preferred response?

For contrast, we could then ask our adolescent what he thinks of craftsmen who combine functionality with beauty. Then on to artists who specialize in beauty — some solely for the purpose of making money — others for enhancing their connection to being alive. We could also explore scholars — some lost in ideas, while others study life in order to understand and enhance it. Or, is there any combination of life's options that our adolescent would like to explore or imitate?

This is one example for how to explore life's options and use the information to identify purposes we can respect and admire, and might want to learn from, or imitate. Engaging in this conversation with an adolescent would create a warm and satisfying experience, would constitute pursuing truth, and would add insight to anyone's understanding.

One part of helping an adolescent explore life's options and character traits that can be satisfying for parents is they too have the opportunity to re-explore life's issues and re-define themselves. It is important to note that part of being intimately and actively connected to life, rather than being lost in passive entertainments, is that we continue to explore and discover life's external options and desirable character traits throughout our existence. This process is needed if we want to redefine our priorities and purposes as we learn from experience what is critical to creating a meaningful life.

For example, in leading adolescents we may see that our lives have been spent becoming successful in our careers and insuring financial security, so our first priority has been to complete functional goals. Now, in exploring life with our adolescent we may decide that it is time to make some changes. Perhaps, we may see a need to carve out time for more experience in nature, or with music and art, or learning about how other people have responded to life by reading biographies. We may even learn that the whole internal dimension of human life is something we just assumed we understood, but now begin to see is a vast new world that we have only just begun to explore.

Of course, one important lesson for both adolescents and parents is that anyone who wants to learn, at any stage of life, must first understand and integrate the critical character trait of *innocent curiosity*. For our curiosity to be innocent it must be our purpose to always expand the edge of our own understanding, as opposed to create conclusions that are by definition end points that shut down all further exploration. *Nothing kills curiosity, and with it the ability to learn, quite so effectively as the sadly ubiquitous, "I already know that!"*

At the core of pursuing truth and developing wisdom is being relaxed with a state of ignorance, and totally innocent in our curiosity to constantly expand the breadth, depth and detail of our skills, insight, understanding and wisdom. If we lead adolescents into learning how to explore reality and discover truth motivated by innocent curiosity, we will help them acquire the basic character traits necessary to create a lifetime filled with lasting satisfaction and real meaning. Since a lifetime of growing requires a constant supply of energy, we will now explore life's Artesian well of renewable energy — experiencing beauty.

Experiencing Beauty

The ultimate purpose in the normal world is to *enjoy* life. In this framework, the purpose of beauty is pleasure, and frankly, there is nothing *wrong* with this purpose. The only problem is that pleasure does not feed a real internal need, and provides no real meaning or lasting satisfaction. On the other hand, if we pursue beauty for the purpose of creating an *innocent sensual connection* to being alive, then we will not demean the experience of beauty into mere pleasure, but will respond to beauty with a feeling of *pure joy*.

We all need the innocent experience of pure joy to renew our energy and optimism. Without the joy provided by experiencing beauty, the effort necessary to master love and wisdom, as well as the inevitable trials, pains, and losses of ordinary life can feel like too much, and we often respond by escaping into empty pleasures and futile distractions.

Escaping into pleasure and distraction is what anyone can observe is the response of most normal Americans to the stress of everyday life, and adolescents are in the vanguard of the cultural stampede to escape reality thru distraction. Our choice is to be swept up in the cultural stampede over the cliff of distraction, or consider the possibility of teaching ourselves the real joy and lasting satisfaction of providing a daily experience of innocent beauty.

As parents, our motivation to chart a course away from the herd, even though it requires effort and we occasionally feel a bit nerdy, is because we see our own need to have an innocent source of energy and optimism that will help us consciously engage life with enough whole-hearted caring that we want to *express love, pursue truth and develop wisdom.* We also add the motivation of wanting our children to have the opportunity to experience not just a pleasant life, but a fulfilling and meaningful life, which requires we teach them how to understand, experience, and respond to beauty.

Another motivation for teaching our children how to integrate beauty into daily life is that it offers opportunities for learning and sharing that create genuine internal warmth, and a lasting emotional bond. Two experiences we all need. What do you suppose makes everyone avoid the experience of joy, which they truly need, and instead join the stampede for pleasure and distraction?

The answer is simple. The experience of joy is intense and *out of control*, whereas the experience of pleasure is by contrast mild, and feels *under control*. As a result, our control oriented culture prefers pleasure to joy, superficial sentimentality to real love, and cockamamie fantasies and beliefs to developing wisdom. If we want to change these sad preferences, then parents must become leaders by first changing their own purposes and priorities. Personally, I don't see any other way, children rarely teach themselves.

Where do we find universal experiences of great beauty? Nature is a good place to begin. Although fading fast, there are still remnants of nature where we can experience the primal beauty and tender innocence found in wildness, and acquire insight into the mystery and wonder of being alive.

There is overwhelming beauty in ordinary grass, trees, water, wildflowers, birds, and a clear blue sky. In becoming *consciously receptive* to Nature our senses are filled with light, color, sound and the ceaseless motion of a constantly changing world, and in each moment we feel the joy and terror of being alive. We need Nature to create an *innocent sensual connection* to life, love, quintessential moments and real joy.

Compare a moment in Nature with an evening concert of ear shattering sound muffled only by drugs or alcohol, but providing what everyone acknowledges is a *"great time!"* If we listen to what adolescents say about their own music, we will hear they do not use the word *beautiful* to describe it. Instead, the phrase adolescents most often use to describe music they prefer is, "I like the beat." Other than that, they like the excitement of the concert and mingling with all the other adolescents, the stimulation of the sound, and getting high with their friends — beauty is not part of the equation.

In fact, if we look at most modern art and music, no one even pretends its purpose is to be beautiful — or meaningful. Mostly, the purpose of modern music and art is to be distracting, shocking, stimulating or profitable, but not *beautiful.* So if we want to find beauty in music, art, literature, in universal truths, innocent expressions of love, or in wisdom that is timeless, we have to pursue it on our own. We will never find beauty, love, or wisdom by following the herd. Instead, if we want our children to experience beauty, we must first chart an authentic and original course away from the herd, and then be willing to lead.

Understanding Adolescent Sex

A normal adult attitude toward adolescent sex is similar to the attitude toward adolescent drug use, "How do we *control* it?" This is to be expected since adults normally just assume they already *understand* sex: after all, sex is about the two p's—pleasure and procreation—right?

In terms of controlling sex we have two major methods of attempting to control it. The first is the liberal method. We simply accept the inevitable and see to it the little dears can get birth control. The second is the conservative method, always less humane, as well as unrealistic—just get them to say no! Same method as for drugs, and just as ineffective.

No one even attempts to *understand* adolescent sex. What's to understand? Raging hormones combine with large numbers of the opposite sex in close proximity, and voila! lots of sex is the expected outcome. Actually, there is much to understand about sex, in both adolescents and adults. First, raging hormones are only part of the adolescent drive to have sex. Curiosity is another part of that drive. Curiosity about one's own body, as well as curiosity about the physical form and function of the opposite sex.

More important than either hormones or curiosity, is a lifetime of experiencing *internal coldness* from our parents, teachers, and even peers (in the case of our peers we rarely see it). By the time we are teen-agers, we are desperate for emotional warmth that we believe exists when being physically close, or engaged in sex. It is our *internal hunger* for emotional warmth, physical touch, and in general feeling special that really drives the intense teen-age *desire* for sex. The hormones and curiosity are added sources of energy, but not the generic source of what drives us over the edge.

Today, kids learn about sex from the internet and become sexualized at a very young age—way too young for them to have any hope of understanding what is happening. I talk with kids who started having sex at around 13 and by the time they are 16 they are already jaded and cynical, and freely express that sex has no connection with love, and in fact, tell me they do not believe love even exists, in part, because they have never seen any examples of real love they can truly respect and admire.

My point is that kids will be less sexualized, in spite of the internet, if their parents are competent to offer internal warmth, external affection, and guidance into how to create innocent sensual experience through Nature, beautiful art and music, literature, conscious thought and meaningful conversations. The problem for both adolescents and adults is that neither one has a large variety of sources for sensual experience that creates emotional warmth, so everyone is suffering from hungers he can neither define or feed.

The solution people normally rely on is to depend on sex and distraction for their sensual experience, and when both are impersonally engaged, and with no conscious purpose, neither one can even be satisfying, much less meaningful. My advice, for what it's worth, is to first master and then provide emotional warmth through *meaningful conversation*.

Meaningful Conversation

Conversation is an *external expression* of *internal thoughts,* and is the most traveled bridge between one lonely island of human life and another. If our internal thoughts are the normal chaotic and confused tangle of self-absorbed beliefs, feelings and fantasies, then our conversations will not only fail to be meaningful, they will be tedious and tiresome.

If we are of a more practical bent and define life in terms of solving problems, insuring financial security, and talking about our vacation trips, restaurants, movies and TV programs, we may be less chaotic and fanciful than our more *spiritual* brothers and sisters, but our conversations will be just as impersonal, trivial, tedious and tiresome. To be truly meaningful, conversation must fit certain universal criteria.

For instance, to offer meaningful conversations we must choose topics that on some level are truly *worth caring about.* This means the topic must have significance in terms of our needs and potentials, conscious purposes, or pose a question about life, love, or some ordinary event we want to explore, understand, and share.

This does not mean we cannot gossip, talk trivia, or discuss the weather. It does mean that if all we talk about are trivial topics, our conversations will be trivial monologues that only increase our isolation and loneliness. What I see is that by the time children become teen-agers most have zero experience with meaningful conversations, and one result is they are desperately hungry for emotional warmth.

Without the emotional warmth provided by meaningful conversations children are pushed into adolescence with no preparation in how to observe facts, organize their thoughts, think for understanding, articulate clearly, and then share life and love. Instead, they are often confused, isolated, and inadequate to think or talk with a clear purpose or point, certainly not about any internal event, need or potential, and are desperate for focused attention and emotional warmth, as well as for understanding what makes life meaningful.

Adolescents need parents who can lead them into truly meaningful conversations about life, love, wisdom, truth, beauty, how to relate to the opposite sex, think for understanding, and care with a whole-heart. These are standard issue developmental tasks all adolescents need to complete to be internally fulfilled, and over time, create lasting happiness. Leading teenagers into meaningful conversations requires parents who are internally developed, and *therein lies the rub*, as Shakespeare might have playfully phrased it.

The good news is that if we learn how to lead adolescents in meaningful conversations, we can offer the same to our mates, which provides a basic requirement for long-term intimacy and emotional bonding. The bad news, as always, is that we have to work very hard to become competent at offering and receiving meaningful conversation. Part of the work is in learning how to choose meaningful topics, and then explore each topic to the *point of understanding*. Of course, we need to notice that **Understanding helps us learn what is true and needed — but never gives us control.**

<u>Part Three</u>

Developmental Tasks

For Adults

Understanding
Adult Tasks

We need to see that mental and emotional development for human beings is a lifetime process. In the normal world, internal growth is often seen as a task we complete early in adulthood, at about the same time as we acquire a home and family and become externally successful. Of course, people love to say, "I learn something new every day!" but then never identify just what they are learning, or precisely what new skills they are acquiring, or what difference their learning makes in the degree of satisfaction and meaning they are competent to create in everyday life.

Bottom line, when people continue to learn in adult life it is almost entirely about external information pertinent for playing the game of *Trivial Pursuit*, but totally useless for enhancing self, life, and other-awareness, or building skills necessary for personal fulfillment, emotional bonding, and professional satisfaction and meaning.

The information and skills we need for internal development requires that we change from being *control/belief and feeling-based* to becoming *observation-based*. Once we make this shift **and** master the ability to apply a *scientific attitude* toward understanding every internal and external dimension of human life, we are prepared to learn. We will still not have learned anything, but we are *prepared to learn*!

The key for adults to be *prepared to learn* is to successfully complete child and adolescent developmental tasks. If we complete our child and adolescent tasks, we enter adulthood competent to provide *emotional safety* and *self-worth*. We will also have developed an *accurate self-awareness* and will have the skill to *explore* any event, internal or external, and *discover* what is true and needed. Not only will we master and integrate these skills, but we will also have created a mental foundation for defining the kind of person we want to be, and the character traits we want to develop.

In addition, we will have a sense of what is required to create professional satisfaction and meaning, not just how to pursue a secure or financially rewarding job or profession. Finally, we will have learned a bit about intimacy and emotional bonding, how to offer meaningful conversations, and how to think for understanding and care whole-heartedly. This pretty much completes the foundation we need for entering our twenty's prepared to learn about life, as well as define and master the first level of our adult tasks.

The only *fly in the ointment* is that I have never met a live person who has completed all their tasks by the age of 20 or 21, or anything close. The consequence is that most people enter adulthood at a disadvantage, because they are never taught they have developmental tasks, and as a result, are condemned to muddle thru without completing a single one. I bring this up to emphasize the fact that development is a *sequential learning process*, which means that each internal task is critical to successfully completing the next level.

The key to completing our developmental tasks is to first *observe* they exist. Second, we must *define* each one in detail. Third, we need to *study* the critical information and acquire the necessary *awareness and skills*, and fourth, we need to *practice* until we successfully complete each internal task. Following this process will guarantee success in any pursuit, internal or external. Many people understand this process as it applies to the pursuit of approval, academic success, sports, or for a profession, but don't feel they should have to work so hard for internal fulfillment, intimate relationships, or professional satisfaction and meaning.

Once we understand that a satisfying and meaningful life based on fulfilling our internal human potentials cannot be reduced to simplistic ideas, beliefs, feelings or techniques, and we decide that we want an internally fulfilled life, then it's time to suck it up and commit the energy and effort. Or, we can decide that internal development is *too much work*, and either give up entirely, or find one of a zillion self-help gurus who have *easy answers* and *quick fixes* for every issue.

For anyone still reading, we will now identify the critical issues and developmental tasks facing every one of us as we march thru our unique lifespan. We will define the tasks as they expand and change with every decade of life. This approach of defining developmental tasks by decade will help to create an overall *vision of life* so necessary to understanding ourselves and the mystery of being alive in the context of a *big picture*. Normally, we move through life unconsciously reacting to the moment, and never do develop a *big picture*.

Dr. Paul Hatherley

The Twenty's — Decade of Immortality

We have seen that adolescence is a *time of transition*, and the twenty's are a decade of exploring and experimenting, defining ourselves on every dimension — personal, relationships, and professionally — while thru it all we feel immortal. Physically, I am told we reach our peak at 25 (it's a slow downhill after that!). We also mature mentally and emotionally in terms of our capacity to think and care, but if we want to fulfill all our human potentials, we need to spend the rest of our lives developing our internal awareness and skills.

With normal training we tend to peak out in every way in our twenty's — thirties at the latest. By contrast, with the training required for internal development, we continue to expand our ability to *think for understanding, express love, develop wisdom and experience and create beauty* for the rest of our lives. The problem with normal training is we circle every neurotic issue and incomplete task through each stage of life and lose value as we age, but if we learn how to become conscious, caring and internally competent, we gain in value over our entire lifespan. Which process would you prefer?

The conscious purpose for exploring and experimenting in our twenties is to learn what life offers, what is possible, and what we prefer. We also need to build on what we started in adolescence by identifying the character we have, and the one we want to develop. Next, we need to *discover* our role and responsibility in relating to the opposite sex, and we need to *experiment* until we find a profession that fits.

Our twenty's is the time when we do an apprenticeship or acquire training to learn a trade or craft, or attend college and experiment with different majors to discover what is both appealing and fits our talents. It is a time when we need to *explore* life through personal observations, books, movies, teachers and peers to discover the options life offers, what other people have chosen and the consequences, and what we want for the *big picture* that defines our entire lives, as well as the *little picture* that defines the immediate present.

In today's world where education and everyday life is so expensive, and the competition for jobs and professions is so intense, it is hard for young people to *explore and experiment.* Instead, young people today feel intense pressure to select a life's work based on being anxious to succeed in creating a secure and well-paying future, rather than take time to find what fits their talents and will be satisfying and meaningful in the long-term.

My model for how to approach my twenty's came from observing famous people from the 18th, 19th and early 20 centuries. What I saw was that many famous writers did not attend college, but instead spent their twenty's exploring life to acquire experience they could use to gather material for their writing. So Mark Twain became a riverboat pilot and wrote about his **Life On the Mississippi**, and Stephen Crane put his life in danger many times to gather the experience that lead to writing **The Red Badge of Courage.** John Muir tramped all over the United States and became a naturalist, famous writer, and fierce protector of Nature's splendor.

In addition, Abraham Lincoln, based entirely on what he described as nothing more than a *year of formal schooling*, became a lawyer, politician, president, and world famous icon for intelligence, caring, and integrity. To accomplish these tasks required that he self-educate through reading books and teaching himself how to think for understanding. Also, as we have seen, Lincoln knew that he wanted to make a contribution to the *collective human experience*. Since he felt it would need to be through politics, he practiced alone talking to an *audience of trees* to develop his oratorical skills.

Using these models and many more, I consciously explored life during my late teens and throughout my twenty's. I began with two years in the military, which was more than enough to experiment with and eliminate that option! When released from the military, I was still only 19 and began exploring life in a leisurely and long college career.

During my years as an undergraduate, I experimented with majors in physics, business management, English literature, history and philosophy. Eventually, I wound up with a major in English and two minors in history and philosophy. I went to graduate school for a secondary teaching credential but dropped out six weeks before completing it because I felt totally inadequate to *understand* the students. I was to regret this decision until after I completed my Ph.D. in psychology and had a flourishing private practice.

The value of all this exploring and experimenting is that along the way I was learning about human life, what other people had done, what was meaningful, and what was not!

After dropping out of the teaching program I went to work for several corporations in management trainee positions. In this experiment, I worked for Bank of America, California Federal Savings & Loan, and California Casualty Insurance company. All three American corporations were governed by a conscious purpose to make money and exploit people, and all three offered its employees a similar stultifying experience of life at its most mediocre and dull. After this corporate experience, I was clear that if I could not find a niche in life that I could genuinely love, then it was time to put a bullet in my brain because life working for a corporation, for me, was worse than death.

Suicide may seem a little extreme to some, but for me this was a step toward self-definition that was quite freeing. Admittedly, in addition to freeing my mind it also created a lingering depression that lasted until I found my niche in Psychology where I could grow in understanding, give to other people, and make a living. This combination of being free to grow, give, and make a living was my life's dream, though for a few years I despaired of ever fulfilling it.

While my path to a satisfying career was more intense than some, acquiring a model for *how to explore*, the *external opportunity to explore*, and the *awareness that exploring is necessary* to discover what fits our purposes and is worth respect and admiration so it is something we can genuinely love, is part of an ongoing process of defining ourselves that we all need to master, not just for our twenty's, or just for a career, but for our entire lives as we continue to grow and change.

Personal Development

In addition to exploring life and discovering what we need to create a satisfying and meaningful career, the twenty's are also a time to define our personal lives, or what we need to fulfill ourselves, all alone. People have always spent their twenty's working on creating a career, but today, discretionary time is often spent by hanging-out with friends, traveling, drinking, partying, and generally rewarding ourselves for the day's labors by entertaining into oblivion.

While we never notice it at the time, our twenty's are when we establish patterns that define the rest of our lives. Normally, we divide life into two sections: work and play. Work is what we do to make money and to maintain ourselves, home, and family, and play is how we reward ourselves with pleasant distractions.

Rarely does anyone see that our twenty's are when we need to explore life to discover lasting interests that connect us to the mystery of being alive, enhance daily experience, and provide opportunity to master the activities and awareness necessary to create a truly fulfilled and meaningful life. It is also rare to see that once we establish a habit *pattern* of working for money and maintenance, and playing for distraction and pleasure, that we leave no room in our lives, and create no file in our minds for learning how to *express love, pursue truth, experience beauty or develop wisdom.* One sad consequence is that we unintentionally create impoverished internal lives, and never even notice!

Following the example of famous people from previous centuries, and my own model of wanting to be both a man's man and a woman's man, I used my late teens and twenty's to learn about life and master skills. For instance, in learning to be a craftsman, I taught myself carpentry and car mechanics. In becoming a scholar, I pursued history, philosophy, business, economics, literature, politics, psychology and science, as well as religion and Eastern spiritual practices.

My purpose was to visit everywhere the human mind had gone in my attempt to understand the mystery, wonder, and terror of just being alive. I also wanted to be a man who could work with his hands, so I could build furniture to my own taste, or repair my car and be as much as possible functionally independent. Of course, in making this choice I did not have much time for partying. There is no way anyone can do everything. Life is limited to twenty four hours per day, no more no less, so it's imperative that we set priorities.

Another interest that I developed in my twenty's was to teach myself how to read music and first play the electronic organ, and then the piano. I even took lessons for a year or so, until eventually I faced the fact that I lacked talent, and shifted my attention to be a "great listener to classical music" rather than a mediocre to poor performer of popular music. My interest in classical and some forms of popular music has been a lifetime source of *innocent sensual experience* that has provided a deep well of beauty, energy, and inspiration.

During this decade I also took up backpacking and spent from three days to two weeks alone in the wilderness. These experiences brought me face to face with the fear of being alive, alone, and out of control as I waded thru long lonely nights far from people, modern conveniences, and feeling safe. I developed a love for the adventure and loneliness of being more than three days into the high Sierra's knowing I could not walk out in a day, and being *voluntarily committed* to work thru whatever came up — positive or negative.

The interests I began in my twenty's have grown with me over a lifetime and provide *warm connections* to my experience of being alive. So now, today, perched on the cusp of old age, I have a long and loving relationship with Nature and classical music and its composers, and find myself on a first name basis with the world's greatest minds — all dead!

Though physically long gone, the people I am closest to live on — as Anne Frank was determined to do — through the legacy of their lives, their contributions to the collective human experience, and the written words that so meaningfully articulate their conscious experience of being alive.

My vision for the future is for human beings to develop our collective minds and emotions, so the warm connections I experience with the marvelous minds of past and present, people can learn to create in everyday life, and the intimacy that comes from sharing innocent and honest connections to ordinary experience will for the first time be available to all.

To turn this vision into reality requires that we observe daily experience and take in the experiential fact that without *intimacy, intelligence, innocence and honesty*, human life is futile, but with these developments, we can all be fulfilled.

Romantic Relationships

The first thing I learned in my twenty's — and life has consistently reinforced — is that *relationships are difficult.* Not breaking news for anyone, and the reasons are many. The most significant reason that creating intimacy is and always has been extremely rare and difficult is that most people lack the *internal development* necessary to be a satisfying mate. This is a bottom-line obstacle that has seemed irresolvable.

Seeing that intimacy is rare may at first feel depressing, but when we learn this problem is caused by the fact that people are *developmentally incapable* of being intimate, we have good reason to be optimistic, because with the information in this book we now have clear definitions for all the developmental tasks in each stage of life. Armed with clear definitions, we are prepared to understand and complete our developmental tasks and grow into being an internally competent adult *developmentally capable* of intimacy.

It would have been helpful if this information had been available when I was an adolescent, so I would have had a chance to create intimacy and meaning in the confusing and tangled world of romantic relationships. As it was, my relationship life began at sixteen, with Bonnie, my first love.

This first relationship was extremely important, in part because it was so innocent, and even in our state of perfect ignorance was non-neurotic, straight-forward, honest, and fed our hungers to be acknowledged, desired, appreciated and touched: physically, mentally and emotionally.

Bonnie and I did not fit together in the sense of being plausible mates for life. I was in advanced college classes, and Bonnie was in the more remedial track and did not graduate. One consequence was that Bonnie had a vision of what she wanted from life that was traditional, but quite different from mine. What we did share was a genuine respect for each other, an innocent hunger for warmth and affection, and a heroic capacity to make-out for hours!

These points are significant because in my extensive lifetime research into what, *if anything,* will create true intimacy, I discovered that IQ and academic achievement are **not** critical variables. I also discovered that it does not matter if someone is pretty or plain, voluptuous or athletic, rich or poor, extrovert or introvert, or any of the characteristics that in normal life we usually expect either do, or should matter.

Instead, Bonnie showed me that being non-neurotic and innocently honest are the fundamental pre-requisites for true intimacy, no matter what someone's IQ, degree of physical attractiveness, or level of achievement. I also learned that building on the pre-requisites and creating a life-long mate relationship is more complicated than the experience of simple intimacy, and requires a degree of internal equality and parallel purposes that Bonnie and I did not share.

Nonetheless, what we did share fed important internal hungers we could never have satisfied on our own, and this made a permanent and life-affirming difference for us both. Bonnie and I dated for almost two years and our relationship came to an amicable, and sad close after I joined the military.

One significant lesson I learned from my relationship with Bonnie came about twenty years later, shortly after the class reunion that Bonnie attended and I did not. Bonnie called me ostensibly to inquire how I could be so rude as to be in town and not come to the reunion. I was 37 and single, and Bonnie was 38, and divorced with two children, and we decided to catch-up on twenty years of events over dinner.

We both had a good idea of how the evening would go, so neither one was surprised when after dinner we ended up in my bed. I was on my right side cradling Bonnie's head in the crook of my arm looking into her eyes. We were both shocked at how relaxed and natural we felt being together, and the ease with which we reconnected after twenty years, like it was only yesterday that we had last seen each other, rather than what in hindsight felt like a previous lifetime.

Underneath our relaxation and ease was a tidal wave of longing and hunger that we purposefully restrained, so we could savor the moment. Then, with our eyes softly and intimately connected, Bonnie said, "I'm really going to enjoy this!" The honesty in her statement perfectly mirrored my own feelings, but took me totally off-guard by the degree of innocent vulnerability I knew I could not match. Tears instantly welled-up in my eyes, and in just a moment, one fell.

When that tear struck her cheek, Bonnie and I lost our restraint and the tidal wave we had consciously held back was suddenly released in an irresistible wave of energy and passion sweeping us into an experience that was agonizing in its sweetness and satisfaction. Indeed, Bonnie was right!

By contrast, for a time in high school I had another girl friend who definitely fit the genius category. She too called me around the same time Bonnie did, only to say she was in town visiting her parents and wanted to catch-up. In listening, I soon learned that Janet was working as head honcho (technical term) running the defense department's primary computer center located underground in the basement of the Pentagon. She had married an experimental psychologist who was working at a local university, and had two kids.

I suggested that I come over for a few minutes and visit with her and her parents. Janet immediately demurred for a strange reason. She said she was afraid that old and overly friendly feelings would be awakened, so I joked that with her parents present we would be properly chaperoned, but she made it clear that it was not funny. After all the time that had passed it was clear to me that her connection with the experimental psychologist was a bit lacking in passion, and she was genuinely afraid to awaken old hungers.

The point of these two stories, both occurred outside the twenty's, is they helped me understand the often perplexing romantic experiences that did occur in my twenty's. Not only did they help me understand my own romantic dilemmas, but more important they helped me understand the *universal* dilemmas that I observed in my psychology practice almost everyone seemed to suffer from to one degree or another.

For instance, my interactions with Bonnie were always clear, innocent, straightforward and satisfying. By contrast, with Janet interactions were always complex and tangled.

The reason for this difference was that Bonnie did not suffer from the basic insecurities, self-doubt, and desire to be in control that Janet did. The fact is all three of us were hungry for warmth and affection, but Bonnie and I were honest about the pain and receptive to innocently feeding our hungers, whereas even in high school Janet was always trying to hide her hungers, even though she was, as most kids are, desperate for warmth and affection.

One lesson is that when we fail to complete our childhood developmental tasks then intense hunger for emotional safety and self-worth will distort every interaction. Another lesson is that when we choose *control* over *understanding*, nothing can ever be simple, innocent or straightforward, and we will always be in competition with the people we love. *The reason is that only one person at a time can be in control, or get their way, and when we choose control we compete with all the other control freaks (almost everybody) for who will be in charge of getting what he/she wants today!*

By contrast, when it is our purpose to understand, we easily share this goal, or desire, so our interactions with the people we love become co-operative rather than competitive. The reasons are simple: one, we share a conscious purpose; and two, the experience of understanding creates closeness, while competing for control makes us adversaries. Nothing is more critical to the happiness of individuals and couples than choosing to pursue understanding rather than control.

In struggling to connect with romantic relationships in my twenty's, I learned that what I shared with Bonnie was rare. I soon discovered that everyone I met, no matter how smart, educated, or accomplished, suffered from a lack of emotional security and self-worth that made conscious sharing either difficult, or impossible. To me it seemed irrational for women who were beautiful, smart, educated and accomplished to be handicapped by a lack of self-worth, so I kept searching, thinking there must be someone who would be relaxed, innocent, self-assured, and available for intimacy.

Eventually, I discovered that only a few people manage to complete even childhood tasks. One consequence is that few people fulfill their personal potentials, and even those who do rarely find someone with a similar development. As a result, truly intimate and passionate long-term romantic relationships are exceedingly rare. You can confirm this sad perception by observing the people in your small circle and start counting those couples who even seem to be internally developed, personally fulfilled, and emotionally bonded.

Adult Tasks—
Thirty's & Forty's

In childhood, our parents lay the mental and emotional foundation that will define us for a lifetime. In adolescence, we have a chance to modify that foundation, for better or worse, before we transition into adulthood. Then, in our twenty's we lock in our response to life thru career, mate, and lifestyle choices, and by adopting normal attitudes and purposes that become permanent fixtures in our characters and personalities.

By the thirty's most people who are going to have families have either already started, or seriously get down to business. For most people, the thirty's are a time when they establish a marriage, build a home, start a family, and further their career. If there is one word that defines our thirty's, that word would be *busy*! Not only are we busy, but we are normally one hundred per cent *externally* focused. Few people in their thirty's have the time, energy, or desire to focus on *internal* development.

For many people, in part because they are busy *building* a home, marriage, family and career, the thirty's feel like a happy time of life. The only problem is that without internal development, we inevitably plant the seeds for unhappiness. Discontent is caused by a lack of intimacy with our spouses, unhappy children, and little or no meaning in our own lives.

Understanding vs. Control

At each stage of life we have a chance to make changes, or *stay the course*. Most people choose to stay the course because human beings feel secure keeping with the familiar, rather than moving toward something new. This is a problem since *internal development* requires we first see we have been raised to want *control,* and then that we need to *change* this normal response to consciously pursue *understanding*.

The desire for control begins instinctually in childhood when we want our lives, parents, and homes to be familiar and predictable, so we can feel emotionally safe. This basic desire is so strong that even if our home-life is painful, we prefer to stay with the familiar, rather than leave it for something that might be much better, but different and unknown. This protective preference often stays with us all our lives.

When we move into our thirty's with a childhood desire for control still forming our response to being alive, then we become *externally* oriented, and our choices are determined by whatever makes us feel most secure. So we choose a mate based on *external or trivial* criteria that we think will provide *control*: for instance, we choose a mate based on appearance, he/she makes us laugh, we have fun together, he/she makes us feel good about ourselves, or we feel safe with him/her.

What we want to *control* is how we feel, our external circumstances, and every outcome. As a result, we make each choice based on external criteria, ignore everything internal, and just hope we will be able to control every outcome.

We apply this formula to our personal lives, marriages, children, and professions. We leave no dimension of life open to the adventure and unpredictability provided by the pursuit of *understanding*: not life, ourselves, other people, or anything we feel is ***deep*** — like internal needs and potentials, conscious life purposes, enduring satisfaction, permanent meaning, or the source of happiness.

When our training is normal, then a *desire for control* rather than *understanding* provides the motivation for every significant life choice from choosing a mate to how we relate to our mate, whether to have children, and how to parent our children. A desire for control also determines our career choices, how we define our characters, and provides the criteria for how we respond to ordinary everyday experiences.

Along with a desire for control comes a vision that life is defined by external criteria. So we think of being alive as an exercise in wanting to feel good, which means we want to control pain and pleasure. This is how every normal person winds up wanting the same things — comfort, pleasantness, security and success. As parents, we teach our children, like mother bears teach their cubs, to want the same things we do, and we teach them by example to avoid, ignore, and remain ignorant of *understanding* internal needs and potentials, conscious purposes, or how to create a meaningful life.

If you see that all internal fulfillment, integrity, peace of mind, intimacy and emotional bonds, creativity, meaningful work, empathy and compassion come from this one choice — would you want to change to *pursue understanding*?

In my thirty-five plus years of counseling and educating, most people have answered this question by choosing to *stay the course* rather than *change*. It has truly puzzled me to offer parents a path to *understanding* that gives them the power to nurture their children into developing emotional safety and self-worth, as well as become internally and externally competent, and have the parents be upset because *understanding* did not give them *control* over their children's behavior.

I have also offered couples a similar power to nurture each other and save not only their marriages, but also their lifestyles, homes, and the integrity of their families, and once again see people be upset that all I offer is understanding, not control. Then, I see people destroy their peace of mind, as well as children's well-being, long-term marriage, lifestyle and even careers over being committed to the *belief* that understanding has value only to the extent it can be used to provide what is in fact, the *illusion* of control.

One consequence is that people will *pervert* understanding for the purpose of control, but not *pursue* understanding for the purpose of nurturing. This is one reason people can work hard trying to master their needs and potentials, or learn how to think for understanding, but make little or no progress, simply because their underlying purpose has not changed from *wanting control over feelings, facts and outcomes,* to *wanting understanding for the purpose of nurturing.*

Once we want *understanding for the purpose of nurturing,* we can master all the internal needs and potentials necessary to fill our lives with satisfaction and meaning.

The Power of Understanding

Everyone wants power, whether they admit it or not. The problem is that few people *understand* power: what it is, or how best to use it. If people did understand power, they would want to understand internal needs and potentials, so they could become competent to nurture themselves, other people, and even Mother Nature. Becoming competent to nurture is a life-affirming power that gives us *influence*, but never *control*. Control is only an illusion, and no one has it.

The influence provided by first pursuing understanding, and then becoming competent to nurture is defined by *acquiring the power* to build intimacy in romantic relationships, help children develop their minds and emotions, and create internal and external fulfillment for ourselves.

During our thirty's and forty's we experience the heart of our adult lives where we are at full maturity on every level: physically, mentally and emotionally. More than ever we need the power provided by internal development to absorb these two decades, and in the process feed our needs and fulfill every potential in this all-important time of life.

Without the power of understanding and the internal development it makes possible, we simply pass thru this period of life *too busy to experience, and too unconscious to fulfill.* Rather than fulfill our potential to create consciousness and caring, we stay busy trying to control pain and pleasure, and we miss-out on the intimacy of emotional bonding. Rather than fulfill our potential to create meaningful work, we focus on making money. In place of learning how to experience and create beauty, we frantically seek superficial pleasure. Rather than teach our children how to love, live and learn, we show them by example how to ignore, deny and avoid. It is important to remember that the information necessary for each step in internal growth is detailed in my five books.

The only problem is that people are trained to want the *illusion of control* rather than the *fact of understanding*, so there is no file in people's brains for valuing or storing the information they need. When we do not value something, and have no file in our brains, then even if that thing is critical for our happiness and well-being, internal and external, for us it does not exist.

This is what we see in American life and culture today: that is, the activities of expressing love, pursuing truth, experiencing beauty and developing wisdom are not valued, and there is no file in people's brains to store the information necessary to develop them, so literally, they do not exist!

I am spending a considerable space on this topic because people have taught me that when they fail to see the value, and feel no *desire* for the power of understanding, then they have no hope of making objectively observable progress toward the internal development of their minds and emotions.

In stark contrast, once people acknowledge the value of understanding, and consciously commit energy and effort to becoming internally competent to nurture, then they learn quickly and completely, so change becomes a valued friend, rather than something they fear and avoid.

Internal vs. External

By the time most people reach their thirty's, their careers are chosen and well-established, or well on the way to being established. In my case, by thirty-one I had completed a master's degree in Marriage & Family Counseling and was licensed as a MFT. However, it was not until I was thirty-five that my Ph.D. was complete, and it took another two years to obtain a license as a Clinical Psychologist. So before thirty-five, I could not even think about finding a suitable mate and having a family. I was way behind the curve!

Normal curves are changing. For instance, as of 2005, for the first time in American history, a full 51% of women over the age of 15 were single because they were either never married, or divorced. I believe this trend continues to expand. The issue is that fewer people are following the traditional path and getting married and producing children in their twenty's, but of those who do have children, the vast majority get the job done by their middle to late thirty's.

Whether or not people choose to have children, the thirty's is when everyone plants the seeds for future fulfillment and happiness, or discontent. This is the time we build on the *internal development* we completed in childhood, teens, and twenty's, or *cement-in* a neurotic life based on *external* experiences — like security and success — that we often try to balance with superficial entertainments and distractions. The problem for everyone, regardless of marital status, is we are trained to build our lives entirely on *external* experience.

What makes the normal external focus a problem is that personal fulfillment, as well as intimacy in relationships and meaning in our professions is built on *internal* experience. *External* needs and desires are important for survival and for creating a *comfortable and pleasant life*, but *internal* needs and potentials are where **satisfaction, meaning, peace of mind, creativity, mastery, consciousness and caring reside**.

Personal Fulfillment

We have seen that life takes place on three dimensions: *personal, relationships, and profession*. With normal training, we all *believe* that if we find a profession that pays well, get married and have a family, or skip the marriage and family and live for approval and pleasure, then we will do the best we can with being alive, and we will be happy. Of course, there are millions of single parents struggling just to survive, as well as millions of individuals drowning alone in this "new economy" where the nation's wealth is defying gravity and flowing upward with all the force of a Niagara falls!

Wherever we find ourselves on the economic continuum, the one *belief* most people share is that an externally pleasant and secure life, where we are free to follow our impulses for the primary purpose of pleasing ourselves, is the ultimate goal of human existence. As a consequence, if we look at the individuals and institutions that define American culture, we see a surprising consensus that says the purpose of life is to provide a comfortable, pleasant, and luxurious existence.

One consequence of this collective consensus about what makes a *good life* is that we have created a culture where few people and no institutions seem to have a speck of integrity, conscious internal purposes, empathy, compassion, or the slightest degree of mental and emotional development. As a result, we cannot view a single institution: politics, religion, business, medicine, or even education with genuine respect and admiration.

Instead, everywhere we look we see people being totally self-absorbed, obsessing about trivial advantages and superficial pleasures, insecure in their self-worth, isolated and disconnected in their relationships, working solely for money, etc. As a result, all our institutions seem without limits in their willingness to deceive, manipulate and exploit for no greater purpose than to try to increase the bottom line yet one more percentage point, get reelected, polish their image, or crush the competition and win more power and pleasure.

For young people in their teens, twenty's and thirty's, this leaves only two options: join the tawdry rush for advantage and approval, or leave the herd and go their own way. The problem is most people have no clue as to what direction they need to travel, or for what purpose, and to what end. What we need are *conscious purposes* for our individual lives that we can truly respect and admire.

Our conscious purposes must lead to creating integrity and peace of mind, while also fulfilling our internal human potential to *express love, pursue truth, experience beauty, and develop wisdom.* This is a vision of life we can all respect.

Dr. Paul Hatherley

A Vision of Internal Life

The people I talk with, no matter what their age or circumstances, have no vision of internal life. This means they come in with *no* understanding of a single internal need or potential in themselves, or their mates, friends or children. Since the people who can afford my services have enough money, the source of their problems is always internal, and since no one has any training in the internal it takes a long time and hard work for anyone to make significant progress.

The younger we begin in acquiring an education into the internal needs and potentials that make us fully human, and are pre-requisites to lasting happiness, the better our chances of fulfilling our internal potentials and creating real satisfaction and genuine meaning. If we complete adult internal tasks by our thirty's, we can teach our children, so the next generation can begin adult life with a degree of understanding and skill unprecedented in human history.

Also, with internal development young families could fulfill rather than frustrate their universal hungers for close emotional bonds that all people long for, but almost no one gets to experience. In the process of growing internally, we elevate our lives and characters to a level of integrity and fulfillment that a few people from the past dreamed would be possible with the development of science and technology, but has not ever actually existed on planet Earth.

A new and conscious *vision of life* makes us pioneers in a grand new adventure—the internal evolution of our species.

We all need the intensity, adventure, and inspiration of being a true pioneer in exploring and expanding the human experience. People in the past explored every geographical nook and cranny of planet Earth, so at this point there is no unexplored space on the whole planet that does not bear scars left by man — be it the ubiquitous trash filling in every space from the depths of the Pacific Ocean to the top of Mt. Everest, or wildlife reduced to a remnant of their former abundance, or landscapes marred beyond recognition, we see the results of man's presence everywhere in Nature.

With internal development, we could feed our *instinctual need to explore and expand* and still preserve the world that is our nest and only home. We need the intensity, adventure, and inspiration that exploring provides, but since there is no new external geography on Planet Earth left to explore, and even though we can continue to explore the scientific world, it should now be clear to everyone that science cannot save us, only mental and emotional development has the power to save us from our own fear, greed, and self-absorption.

Internal development changes our core — consciousness, caring and purposes — and in the process of this change we become competent to understand the complex realities of our internal and external needs and potentials, as well as those of other people and Mother Nature. Right here and now, human beings as a group are astoundingly primitive, which we can observe by seeing that we rely on superstition and painfully simplistic beliefs for making choices critical to our own survival, and the survival of our planet.

For instance, most people *believe* that external success and security, and the comforting pleasantness it provides, will make them happy, even though we have all *observed* in our own families and everyone else's this is not true. We also tend to just assume that *competition* for scarce resources is necessary to drive the economy, provide quality material goods, provide motivation, etc.

We stubbornly maintain this belief in spite of the fact that everyone can observe that *competition without restraint* leads to a ruthless and relentless exploitation of people and resources, and right now has us on the brink of disaster, even though only a few people are clear-headed enough to acknowledge it. If we observed our own history, and the history of the world, we would see that people have relied on competition because they trust that fear, greed, and lust for luxury will motivate people to action.

This is an accurate expectation, the problem is the consequences are poverty and misery for a majority of people, and an exploited and ravaged Mother Nature who at the moment may be using climate change to restore a natural balance that could lead to a drastic *down-sizing* of the human species that created the problem. What we need is enough internal development to create lasting happiness and true internal fulfillment, so finally, we will be *motivated* to work in harmony with both the truth and each other.

It is important to see that being *competitive* is easy, while working *co-operatively* requires internal development—what do you think, is it time for our species to grow-up?

Adult Tasks
Fifty's & Sixty's

We have seen that childhood lays the foundation for our character and personality, adolescence is a time of transition, the twenty's are a decade of feeling immortal while we try to define ourselves further and find a niche in the world. The thirty's and forty's we spend busy as hamsters on an exercise wheel building a home, career, and family. In our fifty's, if we are ever to master our trade or profession, we do it now. The fifty's are also a time when we ripen into maturity and experience internal fulfillment, or suffer from developmental deficits that lead us more into dissipation and decline than internal expansion and fulfillment.

My question about life was: "What must I learn to reach my fifty's and sixty's internally fulfilled, expanding rather than contracting, and vitally connected to the mystery of being alive rather than retreating into distraction or oblivion?"

This question has plagued human beings from the beginning of civilization to present day. Throughout history, people have experimented with various responses to being alive. Some people have gone to extremes to make money, accumulate accomplishments, indulge every pleasure—or deny pleasure and live a monastic existence, or try to create balance by dabbling in all the above. What all our experiments have had in common is they lack *internal development*.

My observations have taught me that without internal development all roads lead to being disappointed with life, and in the end, some feelings of emptiness and futility. The reason is sad but simple, being alive with a mind, body, emotions and life span — and possessing a potential for understanding and self-awareness — is in fact a total mystery. If we pass thru this mystery without developing our potential to understand life and become self-aware, then we miss out on the meaningful elements of the whole experience.

As a result, whatever else we may do — be as rich as Bill Gates, become world famous for our accomplishments, be a *new-age spiritual* buff, be as smart as Einstein, be beautiful or handsome, or blah, blah, blah, ultimately it doesn't matter, because in the face of death, our very own *personal extinction*, no matter what we experience *externally*, without the *internal* dimension it will not be meaningful.

I define *meaningful* as that which has *enduring value*. External activities can be momentarily valuable, but only what we develop internally can provide value that is permanent. This insight needs to be *observed*, **not** *believed*. So observe daily life and note: has money, fun, approval or any external accomplishment lead to lasting value, or permanent meaning? On the other hand, can you see thru observing everyday life that becoming competent to *understand and nurture*, and in the process integrating *love, truth, beauty and wisdom*, will inevitably provide deep satisfaction and lasting value? Can you also see, or imagine, that developing this competence will fulfill your internal potentials, and be *meaningful*?

By the time we reach our fifty's, lifespan starts to take on a new meaning. Now, we are usually long past the feeling of immortality that permeated our teens and twenty's, and even the sense in our thirty's and forty's that life goes on and on, and we have all the time in the world. Finally, we see clear as day that time not only passes, but rather quickly.

The experience of time can be strangely relative. When we are young and looking *forward*, time can seem to stretch on and on toward a long and distant future. From the other end of the continuum, when we look *backward* from our sixty's, time can seem to contract, and to fit into an impossibly small space. Thinking about life span in developmental terms, we learn that time is relative to the *perspective of the observer*, and we see that our unique life span is both long and short, but in the end, shockingly limited.

The fact that life is limited makes internal development, and the ability to create meaning critically important. If we were immortal, time would be irrelevant, because we would have space for every possible experience and option, no rush. With a limited life span, however, we need a *sense of urgency*, not anxiety, just a burning desire to spend our time in life-affirming ways that create lasting value, or meaning.

In normal life, we spend our lifetime pursuing external desires that provide momentary pleasure, or feed our need for survival, but have zero chance to create enduring value. One result is that normal purposes for marrying are for lust, security, because someone helps us *feel good* about ourselves, makes us laugh, or simply provides an entertaining time.

<u>Once Again — Purpose Determines Outcome</u>

With normal purposes we cannot grow, give, or share in our long-term romantic relationships. People often realize in their thirty's and forty's they are unhappy in their marriages, but often wait until their fifty's, when the kids go off to college, before consciously acknowledging they no longer respect each other, have little they share in common, don't want to divorce but don't know how to build something real, intimate, or passionate with each other.

When these couples go to a therapist, or try to fix things on their own, the problem is they do not understand enough about *internal needs and potentials* to be happy in themselves, much less create intimacy with another person. This lack of internal development means they must start at the beginning by first learning how to provide warmth and safety, build self-worth, and learn how to identify significant topics and explore them until they discover what is true and needed.

In other words, we must all complete our developmental tasks in order, and it does not matter at what age we begin, the order is always the same. Mother Nature is very clear on this point, so no matter how rich, smart, educated, or special, Mama Nature allows no exceptions! In normal life, we lack the training to understand internal needs and potentials, so even if we do everything *right* and are well-intentioned and externally successful, in the end we are handicapped by our lack of internal development, so sooner or later we all hit a *wall of discontent* without the skills or awareness to grow.

We can hit the wall of discontent at any stage of life, but our fifty's provides a prime time to notice because we often take a quick moment to catch our breath from the relentless *cycle of routine* and note we really are alive, really are going to die, and then ask, "What the hell is life all about anyway?"

The discontent that motivates this question is based in our personal, relationship and professional lives, and as we have seen, often first comes to light when we feel unhappy with our mates. If we continue to explore, however, it is not long before we notice that somewhere along the line, we lost any *conscious purpose* for our personal and professional lives, as well as our marriage. Now it becomes obvious that we need to re-evaluate our entire response to being alive.

Since normal training teaches us to pursue *control,* and to try to manipulate every outcome for external advantage, it is a change in our life's purpose to shift from wanting control, to feeling a *burning desire* to *understand* the mystery of being alive and become competent to integrate *love, truth, beauty and wisdom* into our minds, emotions, and daily lives. To make this stark change in our purpose requires we *observe* that internal development is the only key to open the door to the lasting value provided by understanding and nurturing.

If we fail to observe this fact, then all our attempts to grow will be in a context of pursuing control. How can we know when our purpose has changed? When we pursue understanding with *total commitment and no conditions.* Now we see that *loving* a mate, child, or even our own lives requires *giving energy and attention with a purpose to understand.*

Once we change our life's purpose from control to understanding, we can start the process of completing internal development beginning with the childhood tasks, and then climb the ladder of development to the point of creating a meaningful life, rather than create a normal life of controlled pleasantness in a tragic context of emptiness and futility.

A New Vision of Life

With a change in purpose, we also acquire a new vision of what life is, and what makes being alive satisfying and meaningful. With a new purpose and vision, we soon see that getting everything we want, being awash in approval, and feeling in control may sometimes be pleasant, but it is never meaningful. So when we are discontent with ourselves, mates, or profession, or all three, and whether we are young and feel immortal, or chronologically mature, *now* is always a good time to begin internal development.

We have already defined the major developmental tasks, so now all anyone needs to do is to study the tasks defined in this book, and explored from different angles and in detail in my other four books, then experiment with daily life until over time all the developmental tasks required at each stage of life are completed. Nothing to it!

One consequence is that if we are committed to working, then our internal development will eventually catch-up with our chronological age. When this happens, we become mentally and emotionally *competent* to express love, pursue truth, experience and create beauty, and develop wisdom.

When we become internally competent is when we *earn our keep* as human beings, fulfill a new internal vision of life, and create personal fulfillment. Now, instead of trying to *control outcomes,* we want to learn what is true and needed in each new experience. So if perchance we should discover to our chagrin that we are fifty and internally unfulfilled, we don't blame our mates, but observe the facts and note what we have already accomplished and what it means to us, and then we *explore* life's options with the purpose of *discovering* precisely what we must *master* to fill-up the emptiness in our personal, relationship, and professional lives.

Now we can see to what degree we have mastered our internal potential to understand perspective — motivations, purposes, needs, wants, behaviors and intentions — our own, as well as everyone else's; including our children, mate, and friends. We also note the consequences to ourselves and the people we love of our internal competence, or lack thereof, to understand internal needs and feed them.

This is where our personal and relationship fulfillment sometimes merge. That is, we may discover that even after going to all the trouble of living with the same mate, or several, and raising children, we have failed to create genuinely intimate and satisfying emotional bonds with anyone. This fact leaves a big hole in many a person's mind and emotions.

While each person's issues and problems contain some unique twists and turns, the resolution for everyone's issues is contained in the process of mastering and integrating love, truth, beauty and wisdom into everyday life.

Expressing Love

We saw in the first chapter on self-worth and emotional safety that *loving* our children begins with *learning* about their needs and unique experience in being alive. Then we saw that *learning* requires we master the ability to *explore and discover* what is true and needed. This sequence of awareness and behavior identifies the first layer in a complex process of *expressing love* — for anything or anyone, including ourselves.

Most issues and problems have their root in our inability to express love. Normally, we are taught to *control outcomes*, which even with the *best of intentions* is the sworn enemy of *expressing love*. This is one reason that real love in normal life is rare, because we are trained to pursue control, and no one is taught even the first step to expressing love.

By our fifty's and sixty's, it is normal to have decades of neurotic habits and conflicts that need resolving and changing due to *believing* that control is good and possible, while also having acquired no *understanding* of internal needs and potentials, and not one specific clue as to how to express or receive love. It is almost never too late to learn, but the clock is seriously winding down and our fifty's and sixty's are the last chance to rescue our lives from what is often a nearly complete experience of emptiness and futility.

Becoming committed to *give* the energy and attention necessary to learn about life, other people and ourselves, so we can feed needs and share the mystery of being alive is one *source of love*, and these two decades are our last chance.

Pursuing Truth

Pursuing truth is the *magic method* for all human growth, be it in science, economics, politics, education, or our own internal fulfillment, emotional bonding, or meaningful work. The problem has been that we have not agreed on a *method* for pursuing truth in any significant human pursuit except understanding nature, an activity we call *science*.

In all other significant human activities we are taught to rely on beliefs, opinions, feelings, assumptions, judgments and fantasies. One sad consequence is that people *believe* that truth in every activity except science is subjective, and cannot be accurately observed and objectively verified. The nearly universal *belief* that *truth* in everything but science is subjective, has kept human beings mentally and emotionally handicapped, and has literally chained us to a *stone-age* level of internal development.

Science itself has only recently (in the last four hundred years) been unchained from the repressive control of religion and allowed to flourish. Now, it is time to unchain all significant human activities by consciously relying on a *scientific attitude* to differentiate *subjective* opinions from *objective* facts in the areas of economics, politics, education and religion, as well as our intuitive beliefs about romance, parenting, and the underlying sources of human happiness.

A scientific attitude can be defined simply as relying on *observations, questions, reason and experiments* to *explore* ordinary experience for the *purpose of discovering* what is true.

Note, a *scientific attitude* employs the *method* every true scientist uses to learn about Nature. If we were to study ourselves using a scientific attitude, we would discover internal needs and potentials, and learn how to define, feed and fulfill them, just as I have done over the past three decades. For instance, we would observe that every child needs parents who can acknowledge and understand him, and every human being needs self-worth and emotional safety, no exceptions. The *no exceptions* part of this statement makes it an *objective fact* we can confirm through observation, rather than a *subjective feeling or belief* that can only be argued.

The important thing about objective facts is they can be observed and confirmed by any sane and rational human being anywhere on the planet, whereas subjective feelings and beliefs only provide fuel for energy-draining arguments and debates. This is one reason that people avoid talking about politics, religion, business practices, economic policies, education, romantic love or parenting skills, because all these activities are considered strictly subjective, (the liberal view) or the province of strict rules of opinion or religion (the conservative view), while both liberals and conservatives deny the relevance and need for a scientific attitude.

It is somewhat amazing that liberals and conservatives agree in *believing* that *objective* reality does not exist in most significant human activities, and then support this stone-age belief with denying the value of a *scientific attitude* in anything except science. Many conservatives still don't accept the value of a scientific attitude, even for science!

My point is that if we want to explore ordinary life and discover what is true so we can understand what is needed, then we must apply the *scientific attitude* to discover in detail what in life is subjective, and what is objective. In applying the scientific attitude, we must first learn about ourselves: for instance, the sources of lasting happiness, how to define and feed our internal and external needs, fulfill every potential, create intimacy and build emotional bonds, and infuse meaning into our everyday lives and relationships, as well as in our daily work and professional lives.

What does this mean to normal people? If we acknowledge the facts of life we see we all want personal fulfillment, as well as security and pleasant distractions, while most of us want a romantic relationship even if we do not have one, and many people have children they need to understand and nurture. Of course, most people try to not only make a living, but also want to derive some degree of satisfaction and meaning from their work.

Each of these significant human concerns requires that we bring a curious mind to the party of life, and then use the scientific attitude to explore the facts and discover what is true. Now, check your memory, did you *explore* the *internal* requirements for being a person, mate, or parent to discover what you, your spouse, or child needed for self-worth and emotional safety, or to be internally satisfied? Or did you have layers of assumptions and beliefs that you unconsciously applied? Most people are laden to full capacity with beliefs and assumptions, but have little or no curiosity.

Experiencing Beauty

One source of the energy we need for loving, learning, and living with intensity and focus is to actively pursue the daily experience of beauty. The key to absorbing the energy and inspiration beauty provides is to consciously pursue her with the innocent purpose of creating a sensual connection to life and love, rather than the normal and often unconscious purpose of trying to exploit beauty for pleasure.

This formula for pursuing beauty works for pursuing just about anything in life — that is, if *we consciously pursue any goal or experience with an innocent purpose, the outcome may not always be what we expect, but it will almost certainly be satisfying and meaningful.*

I began to consciously pursue beauty as a young man. At first, it was mainly because many writers and artists I had read about had valued beauty and I wanted to understand what they experienced and learned, and in general, I wanted to know what all the fuss was about! I began with literature, classical music, and spending oceans of time in Nature — hiking and backpacking alone.

In the process, I saw that in being human I am shockingly *time-limited*, but beauty is *timeless* and fills my senses and mind with satisfying experiences that I respond to with pure delight and genuine joy. I think we need the innocent delight and pure joy from beauty to balance the loneliness, struggle, suffering and loss that sometimes fills-up this often wonderful, but always mysterious experience of being alive.

Developing Wisdom

By our fifty's and sixty's a pure delight in beauty is one experience we can continue to expand, while other things, like our physical prowess, are contracting. Developing wisdom is an internal experience we all need, and is necessary to stay vitally involved with life; in part, because it is something we can continue to expand right up to the last breath. Also, like beauty, wisdom too must be actively pursued, it does not just come to us as a result of growing older.

The only thing that ever *just happens* is that time passes, we age, and eventually, usually sooner than we expect, we pass away. If we choose to pursue wisdom, then we soon learn that of the four internal activities critical to everyone's internal development, wisdom is the last to grow into maturity, mainly because wisdom is a synthesis of love, truth and beauty that over time creates a subtle, deep, broad, and detailed *understanding* of ourselves, life, other people and Nature.

From the understanding necessary for wisdom, we become competent to *love* more genuinely and effectively, and to experience, absorb, and respond to the wonder and sometimes pain of *innocent beauty* more intensely and completely. We also continue to *pursue truth* by the constant addition of new information that we use to edit, revise and expand our picture of ourselves, life and other people. The internal activities of *love, truth, beauty and wisdom* are the only real fountain of youth, vitality, and genuine meaning that life offers.

I say this from the perspective of just having passed thru my 69th birthday, so I speak from a lifetime of observing other people, famous and ordinary, as well as from my personal experience of going thru a nearly complete process of life and living as consciously and purposefully as possible.

My response to being born was to first feel irritated that no one asked for my input on whether or not I wanted this experience! My second response was to admit a power bigger than me made this decision and was not at all concerned about my preferences. My third response was to commit to learning all I could about this perplexing and often frightening mystery of being alive with *a mind, body, emotions, and life span.* I have truly loved this purpose, and the following are a few lessons life has been so kind, and mean, as to teach me.

First, last, and foremost life has taught me there is nothing that offers more lasting value or genuine meaning than the pursuit of love, truth, beauty and wisdom. Second, life has proven over and over that only an *active* response to being alive has any hope of being satisfying, or creating meaning. A passive *wait and see* attitude, or hoping a handsome prince or beautiful princess will fulfill us is totally hopeless.

Only a *conscious purpose* to integrate love, truth, beauty and wisdom can make us conscious, caring and internally competent human beings. Also, only a *scientific attitude* will create internal growth and change—feelings and fantasies never have the power to create true understanding. Last, consciousness and life are multi-dimensional and in constant motion—always complex, never simple.

Appendix

Words to Define for Internal Development

Beginning Words & Phrases:

Internal
External
Needs vs. Wants (Internal & External)
Internal Potentials
Developmental Tasks
Conscious Purposes

Universal Elements of Every Person's Perspective:

Motivations
Purposes
Needs
Wants
Choices
Behaviors

Congruent vs. Contradictory
Acknowledgment vs. Approval

Expressing Love
Pursuing Truth
Experiencing Beauty
Developing Wisdom

Define Scientific Attitude
Observing vs. Believing & Feeling
Describing vs. Judging

Thinking for Understanding vs. Obsessing, Feeling, Believing or Theorizing

Requirements for Human Happiness

Define Self-Worth
How to Create Self-Worth in Adults vs. Children
Requirements for Building Genuine Emotional Bonds

Advanced Words & Phrases

Internal Needs:
    Primal Experience
    Quintessential Moments
    Feed Mind Truth
    Feed Senses Beauty
    Meaningful Work
    Adult Perspective

Internal Potentials:
    Understanding
    Caring
    Mastery
    Creativity
    Contribution

Developmental Tasks for Children:
    Emotional Safety
    Self-worth
    Accurate Self-Awareness
    Skill to Explore Significant Topic & Discover Truth

Developmental Tasks for Adolescents:

Identify with Gender

Consciously Choose and Purposefully Develop Character Traits

Identify Preferences

Create Interests

Learn how to See & Understand Two Perspectives

Separate Satisfaction & Meaning from Pleasure & Approval

Explore Life's Options on Path to Choose Career

Personal Conversation

Conscious Touch

Expand Skill to Explore Significant Topics & Discover Truth

Developmental Tasks for Young Adults: (Twenties)

Adopt Scientific Attitude and Master Thinking for Understanding

Begin to Master Internal & External Needs & Potentials

Continue to Explore Life's Options to Create

Preferences & Life-long Interests

Learn How Other People Have Responded to Life & Note the Consequences

Choose a Mate Based in Part on Sharing Reality, Purposes & Quintessential Moments — As Well as Personal Conversation & Conscious Touch

Engage a Profession or Choose Work that is Satisfying & Meaningful

Developmental Tasks for Middle-Age Adults: (Thirties & Forties)

Master Intimacy in Long-Term Relationships

Master Internal Parenting of Children

Master Seeing & Understanding Own & Other People's
Perspectives

Study & Understand Universal Internal & External
Needs of Human Beings

Study & Understand Needs of Mother Nature

Fully Absorb Role of Adult Human Being Who Gives
Attention & Understanding Without Requiring to be
Acknowledged or Understood in Return

Complete the Mastery of Internal Needs & Potentials

Continue Building *Inventory of Understanding* to Pave
Way to Develop Wisdom

Complete Mastery of Expressing Love (Exploring Love-
Truth-Beauty Continues until Death)

Complete Mastery of Pursuing Truth

Complete Mastery of Experiencing Beauty

Developmental Tasks for Senior Adults: (Fifties, Sixties & Beyond)

Master Role of Mentoring the World (Family, Friends,
Strangers in Need)

Complete Conscious Purposes (Not an End Point—Just
A Satisfying Degree of Completion)

Complete Satisfaction & Meaning in Daily Life (Not an
End Point—Just a Satisfying Degree of Completion)

Become Wise & Integrate It into Character (Doesn't
Mean We Know It All!)

Fully Integrate Love—Truth—Beauty

Contribute to the Collective Consciousness & Caring of
the Human Species

Fulfill Creative Abilities & Accomplishments
(Again—Not an End Point)

Teach Internal Development to Any & All Who Are
Interested

Dr. Hatherley's Books

The Source for finding the definitions for all the preceding words and phrases—and equally important, their application to everyday life--is found in my five books listed below. All books are available on website: **www.paulhatherley.com**

Developmental Tasks for Children, Adolescents & Adults: *A Full Picture of Internal Development from Self-worth & Emotional Safety to Integrating Love, Truth, Beauty & Wisdom*

Master the Science of Living & Art of Being Happy

The Structure of Mental & Emotional Development: *A Precise Path to a Conscious Mind & Whole-hearted Caring*

Expressing Love—Pursuing Truth—Experiencing Beauty: *Three Timeless Steps to the Ultimate Satisfaction—A Meaningful Life*

A Noble Vision of Life